21 Day Abundance Challenge

Gill Hasson

21 Day Abundance Challenge

Plan for a prosperous future

Gill Hasson

First published in Great Britain by John Murray Learning in 2023
An imprint of John Murray Press
A division of Hodder & Stoughton Ltd,
An Hachette UK company

1

Copyright © Gill Hasson 2023

The right of Gill Hasson to be identified as the Author of the Work has been asserted by her in accordance with the Copyright, Designs and Patents Act 1988.

All rights reserved. No part of this publication may be reproduced, stored in a retrieval system, or transmitted, in any form or by any means without the prior written permission of the publisher, nor be otherwise circulated in any form of binding or cover other than that in which it is published and without a similar condition being imposed on the subsequent purchaser.

A CIP catalogue record for this title is available from the British Library

Trade Paperback ISBN 978 1 399 80316 8

eBook ISBN 978 1 399 80319 9

Typeset by KnowledgeWorks Global Ltd.

Printed and bound in Great Britain by Clays Ltd, Elcograf S.p.A.

John Murray Press policy is to use papers that are natural, renewable and recyclable products and made from wood grown in sustainable forests. The logging and manufacturing processes are expected to conform to the environmental regulations of the country of origin.

John Murray Press
Carmelite House
50 Victoria Embankment
London EC4Y 0DZ

www.johnmurraypress.co.uk

Contents

Introduction	vii
Day 1: Understanding abundance	1
Day 2: Understanding your mindset	11
Day 3: Positive, empowering ways of thinking	19
Day 4: Moving away from comparing and competing	27
Day 5: Abundance consciousness	37
Day 6: Knowing your true self	43
Day 7: What do you wish for?	49
Day 8: Visualizing what you wish for	59
Day 9: Identifying your options	67
Day 10: Identifying your attributes	77
Day 11: Getting what you wish for, one step at a time	87
Day 12: Manifesting what you wish for	95
Day 13: Getting started and staying motivated	105
Day 14: Identifying and taking advantage of opportunities	115
Day 15: Giving and sharing	123
Day 16: Having compassion	137
Day 17: Being with positive people	145
Day 18: Being open to receiving	155
Day 19: Simple pleasures and awesome moments	165
Day 20: Having patience in the unfolding of events	173
Day 21: Managing setbacks	183

Introduction

Do you want more from life?

It's easy to think that much of what we have and don't have in our lives is down to situations and circumstances that are beyond our control. It's also easy to look at what other people have and imagine that one way or another, they have more than you and live a life that's better than yours. Perhaps you've wondered what it would be like to be someone who had more in their life: more happiness, more peace, more freedom or more stability. Perhaps you want more money, more success, more fun or more friends.

What if you knew that you could have these things? That you can bring to your life what you really want and wish for?

Well, you can. *21 Day Abundance Challenge* will show you how.

In the first few days of this book, you will learn how to develop an abundance mindset, a way of understanding and thinking about yourself and the world around you that will open you up to a life of abundance. You will learn that with an abundant mindset, you are able to take a proactive approach to life. In a wide range of situations and circumstances, you will be empowered to achieve and attain what you want and wish for.

From Days 7 through to 14 we move on to identifying what exactly it is that you want more of. Whether it's wealth, health or happiness, you will learn about the options, opportunities and possibilities that – one step at a time – will enable you to achieve or attain what it is that you are aiming for.

Once you are on track to working towards what you want and wish for, Days 15–19 support you to maintain and further develop the abundance mindset that will help you move closer to your goals. You will learn how to stay proactive and positive; to make abundance – an abundance mindset and abundance consciousness – a habit.

No matter what happens, we're continually creating our lives; our choices and decisions are what shape our lives. And sometimes we have to make the decision to step back and do nothing. Day 20 explains that sometimes, rather than force things to happen, we just need to go with the flow, to patiently let things be, trusting that things will take their natural course; that there's a time for everything and everything in its time.

Finally, Day 21 encourages you to know that even when you experience difficulties and setbacks as you work towards achieving your goals, there are still options, you still have opportunities to achieve or attain what you wish for. You might just need to take a different direction to get there.

Why 21 days?

Throughout *21 Day Abundance Challenge* you'll be introduced to new ideas and concepts, new ways of thinking and doing. Each day builds on the previous one; as you progress through each of the 21 days, you will see how the different aspects of abundance relate to and inform each other. How, for example, an abundance consciousness relates to and informs small pleasures and awesome things (Day 19). Or how manifesting what you wish for (Day 12) relates to and informs your ability to be open to and take advantage of opportunities (Day 14).

21 Day Abundance Challenge helps you manage the challenge of maintaining an abundance mindset and making it a habit. One day at a time, you will learn new ways to think and behave. Then, after 21 days you'll have established a strong understanding and practice of abundance. And *because* you've spent 21 days practising abundance, you've already started a new habit, a positive, empowering approach that will put you in control and get you more of what you want in life.

How to use this book

Each of the 21 days starts with an aim for the day and a thought for the day. Each day ends with key points and an invitation to set yourself an intention for that day.

INTRODUCTION

There are plenty of explanations, ideas and suggestions to help you understand the principles and concepts that make for abundance.

Every day there are one or more practical exercises for you to do. Some of them are written exercises so you may want to have a notebook or journal to hand for the exercises and your reflections.

The exercises can be easily shared and discussed with others. You may like to go through the *21 Day Abundance Challenge* with one or more other people – a friend, colleague or family member. And, if you belong to a book club, you could suggest *21 Days Abundance Challenge* as a book for you all to read one month. There will certainly be plenty for you to share and discuss at your next meeting!

Whether you work through the 21 days on your own or with others, do begin each day with an open mind; be open to the ideas and suggestions and the exercises you are encouraged to do.

Take on the ideas, tips and exercises with full intention and commitment. Rather than just read and think about them, pour yourself into them. Every day, set aside half an hour or so and fully engage. It's your life that you're creating; you really do have the power to create the life you want.

And finally, it's not a problem if you miss a day. Life happens. Whether you follow each day every day for 21 consecutive days or it takes you longer to cover all 21 days, once you've finished the 21 days, do keep dipping back into the book. Go back to the days that resonated most with you. Then dip in and out of the other days too. As your abundance mindset develops and time goes on, you will find that those become more meaningful too.

There *is* more out there and it's yours for the taking. Go get it!

Day 1
Understanding abundance

INTENTION
To understand the difference between abundance and scarcity.

THOUGHT FOR TODAY
Abundance brings potential and possibilities, opportunities, choices and options.

What does it mean to have abundance? It means having plenty.

Your mindset – your usual way of understanding and thinking about things – may tend towards seeing life and the world you live in in terms of abundance. Or you may be more inclined to view your life and the world in terms of scarcity.

With abundance, there is more than enough. With scarcity, there is not enough.

When you have an abundance mindset, you have a positive view of yourself, other people, situations and events. You're optimistic. In a variety of situations, you expect a favourable outcome. You know that things don't always work out, but if things do go wrong, when there are problems you know you have options and you look for solutions.

If, though, you have a scarcity mindset, you tend to have a negative view of yourself, other people, situations and events. You are inclined to be pessimistic. In a variety of situations, you anticipate difficulties and problems. If and when problems occur, you are likely to resign yourself to having little or no control over your circumstances or what happens next. You see little in the way of possibilities, options and solutions.

DID YOU KNOW?

The origin of the word 'abundance' comes from the Latin word *abundantia*. In ancient Roman mythology, Abundantia was the goddess of abundance, money-flow, prosperity, fortune, valuables and success. She was usually depicted on coins holding a cornucopia (a horn containing food, drink, etc. in endless supply) in one hand and in the other hand, ears of corn. On other coins Abundantia is depicted carrying a cornucopia full of gold coins, which she lets drop behind her wherever she goes.

DAY 1

Exercise: How do you see the world?

One of the first steps to developing an abundance mindset is to be aware of how, in a variety of situations, you usually think about and respond to circumstances and events. Are you inclined to have a scarcity mindset or are you more positive and have an abundance mindset? Below is a range of situations. Read each statement and tick whichever way of thinking or behaving is most likely for you.

1. What comes to mind first when you think back over the last few years?
   a) What's gone well in your life – the things you've enjoyed doing and being part of and the good things that you have.
   b) What you don't have – what didn't go so well; the difficulties and the setbacks you have experienced.
2. You are planning a day out, but something happens that interferes with your plans. Do you:
   a) move on quickly and think of a Plan B?
   b) get stuck thinking how unfair it is and that the day has been ruined?
3. When it comes to sharing what you have with others and being generous, do you:
   a) find it easy – you enjoy giving to others?
   b) find it difficult – you tend to want to hold on to what you've got?
4. You are involved in a work project with colleagues who are not pulling together. Your thoughts are:
   a) We can find a way to sort this out – there has to be a solution that will make things easier for everybody.
   b) These people are a nightmare. This is never going to work out. Why did I have to be involved with this?
5. You'd like to take up a new interest or learn a new skill – a language or a sport, or maybe something to do with music or arts and crafts. You think:
   a) It will take a while, but one step at a time, I'll get there.
   b) There's no point. It will take such a long time to learn and be any good at it.

6. You realize that something is going to take longer than you'd like. Do you:
   a) trust that things will develop and unfold in their own time – you know that there's a time for everything and everything takes time?
   b) get impatient and start looking for ways to hurry things up and try to force an outcome?
7. Someone you know achieves something you'd like to achieve. You think:
   a) I'm inspired! Maybe I could do that!
   b) That will never happen to me – I don't have the same skills/resources/opportunities.
8. Your company plans to dismiss 10 per cent of its workforce on grounds of redundancy. Your reaction to the news is:
   a) I'm going to start thinking about what I might do next – I'll start finding out what other opportunities there might be.
   b) It's bound to be me. It's not going to be easy, finding another job. There's too much competition.
9. You have done something that just didn't work out. You think:
   a) I'm going to learn from this – what do I need to know or do to make sure I don't make the same mistake again?
   b) I screwed up. I'm hopeless.
10. You are choosing from the menu at a restaurant, but there are only a couple of dishes you like or are able to eat. You think:
    a) That's ok. The next meal is only another few hours away.
    b) It's not fair. Why is there such a limited choice?
11. For a while now, you've wanted to work part time so that you can pursue a sideline – write a novel, for example, or study, or train for a new career. Now, thanks to your partner's recent pay rise and their encouragement, you can just about afford to do it. Do you:
    a) start seeing what the possibilities are and begin making plans?
    b) dismiss the idea – supposing the novel is no good, or you can't sing well, or it's difficult to get a job in what you retrain to do?

DAY 1

12. When someone compliments or praises you, you:
    a) find it easy to accept.
    b) find it difficult to accept and feel awkward.
13. When someone you know is struggling in some way, you:
    a) do what you can to help – you know how little it takes for you to make a positive difference.
    b) hold back – you're not sure how to help, or don't want to get involved.
14. A friend tells you they'd like to travel and see more of the world. You think:
    a) With some research, they could see what's possible. Perhaps a working holiday would be an option, for example.
    b) I can't see how they can do that; they don't have the time or the money.
15. When you read your friends' social media posts it seems that everyone is doing well with their lives. You think:
    a) Good for them!
    b) Why is everyone else having such a good time? It just gets me down!
16. You are offered a promotion at work. You'd really like the role. You think:
    a) I don't have all the right skills or knowledge, but I can ask for support and learn what I need to know.
    b) I can't take the promotion. I don't have the right skills or knowledge for the new role.

If you answered mostly **a)**, you are inclined to think in terms of abundance. In a variety of situations, you see potential, possibilities, opportunities, choices and options.

If you answered mostly **b)**, you are inclined to think in terms of scarcity. You see limits, obstacles and blocks. You believe that in a variety of situations, there is little or no choice or few options.

Differences between an abundance mindset and a scarcity mindset

A person with an abundance mindset believes that the world is full of possibilities and opportunities, and that there are few limits to what they can do and achieve. They believe that there are always options and choices and that there's usually more than one way that they can achieve or attain something. A person with a scarcity mindset believes that there are limits to what the world offers and what they can do and achieve.

To help you further understand an abundant mindset and a scarcity mindset, look at the following 12 key differences between the two approaches.

1. An abundance mindset is receptive to new ideas and new experiences. A scarcity mindset is closed off to new ideas and new experiences.
2. When things don't work out, a person with an abundance mindset is accountable and takes responsibility. A person with a scarcity mindset blames themselves, other people or events.
3. An abundance mindset considers what resources and support could help manage difficulties and setbacks. A scarcity mindset doesn't look for or see what resources and support there may be that could help.
4. An abundance mindset is willing to share ideas and information and to support and encourage others. A scarcity mindset is either unaware of the need or is unwilling to share ideas and information, support and encourage others.
5. An abundance mindset is kind, generous and compassionate. A scarcity mindset is either unaware of the times they can be kind, generous and compassionate or they are unwilling.
6. An abundance mindset is aware of and appreciates the good things in their life. A scarcity mindset often fails to recognize and enjoy the good things in their life.
7. A person with an abundance mindset steps out of their comfort zone in order to achieve what they want. A person with a scarcity mindset stays in their comfort zone and settles for less.

8. A person with an abundance mindset is easily inspired. They believe that if someone else is doing it, they can do it too. A person with a scarcity mindset is easily discouraged by other people's success; they believe that if someone else is doing it or has it, there's no room for them.
9. An abundance mindset cooperates, collaborates and negotiates with others and knows that by doing so, everyone benefits. A scarcity mindset is unwilling or unable to cooperate, collaborate and negotiate with others.
10. An abundance mindset sees what there is plenty of, what is going right, what is working now and what may work in the future. A scarcity mindset sees what there's not enough of, what is going wrong, what isn't working and what won't work in future.
11. A person with an abundance mindset learns from mistakes and difficulties. A scarcity mindset has regrets and dwells on missed opportunities and experiences.
12. An abundance mindset is open. A scarcity mindset is closed.

Quite simply, a person with an abundance mindset is likely to get what they want, to achieve and attain the things they set out to have. In contrast, a person with a scarcity mindset is unlikely to achieve and attain the things they'd like to have. They are less likely to get what they want in life.

The good news is that your way of thinking about yourself and the world is not fixed. You *can* learn to think in terms of abundance!

Financial abundance

If you're like most people, a large part of your interest in abundance concerns the possibility of financial abundance. Throughout this book, you will read how abundance can manifest itself in all aspects of your life. You will learn that an abundance mindset is second to none in helping you to achieve and attain what you want, especially financial abundance.

A scarcity mindset involves believing you have little or no power over your circumstances and that you'll never be much better off financially than you are now. You may believe that there are limited options or that you are disadvantaged in some way, that there are circumstances that hold you back from achieving the levels of wealth you desire.

It's important to know that as with any other aspect of your life, staying that way or successfully achieving financial abundance has a lot to do with whether or not you are willing to adjust your mindset and commit to growth.

DAY 1

Key points

- With abundance there is plenty. There is more than enough. With scarcity, there is not enough.
- If you are inclined to think in terms of abundance, you see potential, possibilities, opportunities, choices and options. If you are inclined to think in terms of scarcity, you see limits, obstacles and blocks. You believe that in a variety of situations, there is little or no choice or few options.
- **Set yourself an intention:** Raise your awareness: today, for any decision you make, be aware of the possibilities, the choices and options you have. It could be small decisions, such as what to eat for dinner, or a bigger decision such as how you are going to get something done today. At the end of the day, in your journal briefly describe the situation that needed a decision and what the possibilities and choices were.

Day 2
Understanding your mindset

INTENTION

To better understand your mindset and know that it can change from a scarcity mindset to an abundance mindset.

THOUGHT FOR TODAY
> *The greatest discovery of my generation is that human beings can alter their lives by altering their attitudes of mind.*
>
> *William James*

Whether you tend to think in terms of abundance – you have an abundance mindset – or you tend towards thinking in terms of scarcity – you have a scarcity mindset – it is likely that up till now you've not been aware of the predominant nature of your mindset, or your thoughts and your reactions to events. In fact, your thoughts are so powerful *because* you rarely have conscious awareness or control over them. Your mind simply accepts everything it's 'told' and you respond accordingly.

As we go about our daily lives, our minds are continually thinking, interpreting and assessing our experiences, events and situations. But our brains have a limited ability to process everything that's going on. To make sense of what we experience, we've each developed an 'explanatory style'. This means that when something happens, has happened or is going to happen, our brain makes sense of it in a way that fits with our usual way of understanding events – an understanding that's been influenced by our experiences in life, our upbringing, our family and friends, our environment, education, media influences, religion and culture and so on.

You have a system in your brain called the 'reticular activating system' (RAS) that controls your consciousness. The RAS filters out everything that doesn't support your most prevalent thoughts and behaviour. So first and foremost your mind notices and pays attention to thoughts, beliefs and experiences that match what you already think and believe and have experienced.

If you're more inclined to think negatively – in terms of scarcity – your brain will automatically interpret events in these negative ways. On the other hand, if you're more inclined to positive thinking – in terms of abundance – your brain will interpret and make sense of events in positive ways. Repeatedly thinking in terms of scarcity can lead to a concept known as 'learned helplessness'. This means that, in effect, you 'learn' or 'teach' yourself that opportunities and resources are limited, there's not enough to go round and you have little or no control over your life, other people, situations and events.

Two approaches to the same situation

As you read the scenario below, you will see how one person's positive thinking opens up possibilities and broadens their ideas, whereas

DAY 2

another person's negative thinking limits and narrows their choices, possibilities and opportunities.

Anita and Ben had worked for several years as designers for a furniture company, when they were both offered redundancy. Although it wasn't a brilliant redundancy package, Anita realized that this was her opportunity to work as a freelance designer. She thought about the opportunities and new horizons opening up for her – about how she'd be her own boss, have flexible hours, more control over her days and be free to pursue the type of design work she was really interested in and liked doing. Anita thought about how not having to commute to work would give her more time with her partner and children. Anita drew up a list of agencies and potential clients and asked for advice and information from friends who already worked freelance. She knew freelancing wasn't going to be easy but she identified the potential problems and came up with solutions which included a Plan B in case things didn't work out. Anita was excited about the possibilities opening up to her.

Ben also thought about working freelance, but all he could see were the risks and challenges. Talking to a colleague, he said, 'I don't know how to start setting up my own business and even if I did, I'd be competing with others for clients. Supposing I don't get enough clients, then what would I do?' Even though Ben didn't enjoy working for the office furniture company – he didn't like his manager and he often worked long hours – he turned down the redundancy.

Ben's negative thinking – his scarcity mindset – limits his options and narrows his opportunities and choices. It's a negative dynamic – each negative thought narrows his possibilities and further serves to narrow his thinking. In contrast, Anita's positive thinking creates a positive dynamic: it opens up her mind and broadens her ideas, thoughts and actions. For Anita, each new positive thought prompts further positive thoughts and ideas, an abundance of ideas and possibilities.

It's the same for us all – if you think positively you'll open up your mind and notice opportunities and see possibilities. If, though, you think negatively, your narrow thinking will only allow you to see limits and difficulties.

> ### Exercise: Change your mindset
>
> Get a piece of paper. If you're right handed, use your left hand (your non-dominant hand); if you're left handed, use your right hand. Do the following:
>
> - Draw a square.
> - Draw a circle.
> - Draw a triangle.
> - Write the numbers 1 to 10.
> - Write your name.
> - Write the following sentence: 'I'm writing this sentence with my non-dominant hand.'
>
> This exercise illustrates the difficulty of doing things differently. The same is true about the way you think. Even when you become aware of the way you think – the way you tend to interpret situations and events – it's not easy to think otherwise. But it's not impossible.

Your amazing brain

It helps to further understand what's going on in your brain.

The core components of the brain are neurons – cells that process and transmit information. Neurons are connected to each other by neural pathways and networks.

So, when you think or do something new, a new neural pathway is created. Each time you think or behave in that particular way, your brain uses that same neural pathway. The pathway becomes stronger and stronger each time it's used. It's just like walking through a field of long grass: the more often that path is trodden, the more established the path becomes and the more likely it is that you'll take that path.

This is hugely beneficial to you because it means that if you do something often enough, it becomes automatic – you don't have to think about it. Think of the things you do on a daily basis that your brain and body are so used to that they don't even have to think about it – walking, talking, eating, brushing your teeth, driving, texting, etc.

On the other hand, this same process of neural pathways developing automatic ways of doing and thinking also establishes habits that are not so good for you – smoking, overeating, drinking, negative thinking and so on.

If you often interpret events in a negative way, then you create strong negative neural pathways in your brain. Those neural pathways become so established that they also become habits: negative thinking habits that leave little or no room for more positive, helpful ways of thinking.

All is not lost! The good news is that if you change how you think or what you do, then new, positive neural pathways are formed. When you continue using these new positive pathways, they become stronger and deeper. The RAS in your brain becomes more aware of and tuned in to positive events and possibilities. Eventually, you will have rewired – or reprogrammed – your brain.

So if you needed to learn to use your non-dominant hand to write with, it would take time and effort, because the neural pathway for using your dominant hand is well established. But if you really want to do it, you can forge new pathways and develop a new way of writing with a different hand.

The same is true for anything you want to do or anyway you would like to think. Certainly it takes effort to change the way you think, but it is not impossible and it's never too late!

Exercise: Get out of your comfort zone – rewire your brain

To get used to thinking differently, practise doing something differently. Choosing to break a routine way of doing things on a regular basis can be an effective way to kickstart new ways of thinking, seeing and understanding. Even small changes can help. Try the following:

- Take a different route. Is there a journey you take on a regular basis – to work, to school, to visit family and friends? Try leaving a little bit earlier and taking a different route.

- Do the same at the supermarket. If you have a route that you normally take around the supermarket aisles, change it.
- Change your mode of travel. Walk instead of cycle. Cycle instead of drive. Or get public transport. Take the stairs instead of the lift.
- Change where you sit. At work, sit in a different seat in meetings or for lunch. If you routinely travel by bus or by train, sit somewhere different from where you normally sit.
- Brush your teeth with your non-dominant hand every day for a week.

In your journal, describe what you did differently. How resistant were you to doing something differently? Was it easy or difficult? Write about it in your journal.

It will take time and effort, but if you really want to do it, you can forge new neural pathways and develop the ability to do things with a different hand. You can retrain your brain. It's the same process for establishing an abundance mindset: it takes time, effort and commitment to think in more positive ways but it is possible and it's never too late.

DAY 2

Key points

- If you're more inclined to think negatively – in terms of scarcity – your brain will automatically interpret events in these negative ways. On the other hand, if you're more inclined to positive thinking – in terms of abundance – your brain will interpret and make sense of events in positive ways.
- Once you begin to change how you think or what you do, then new positive neural pathways are formed. When you continue using these new positive pathways, they become stronger and deeper. Eventually, they will replace the old ways of thinking and behaving. You will have rewired – or reprogrammed – your brain.
- **Set yourself an intention:** Today, kickstart new ways of thinking. Choose to do one thing differently. Make it a habit; try to do that one small thing every day for a couple of weeks.

Day 3

Positive, empowering ways of thinking

INTENTION
To move on from limiting thoughts to more empowering thoughts.

THOUGHT FOR TODAY
Turn your face to the sun and the shadows fall behind you.
Maori proverb

Yesterday you will have read that even though you may tend towards a scarcity mindset, your outlook is not fixed. You can learn a new explanatory style – a new way of thinking about and interpreting events. You can learn to think in more positive ways and as a result, experience abundance in your life.

The first step in moving towards an abundance mindset is to be more aware of disempowering thoughts that are part of a scarcity mindset. Once you are aware of how those thoughts may limit and constrain you, you can move on to more helpful, empowering ways of thinking and understanding.

Exercise: Be more aware of your thoughts

Meditation can help train your mind to be more aware of your thoughts. Just follow these simple steps:

- Breathe normally. Focus on your breathing; just be aware of breathing in, then breathing out.
- When a thought arises – which it will – pause and acknowledge it. Say to yourself, 'I've just had a thought.'
- Then return to your breathing.

Simply put aside five minutes each day for this simple meditation.

Replacing negative thoughts with positive thoughts

A mindful meditation practice can help you to be aware of the thoughts in your mind. Then, once you start being aware of your thoughts in everyday situations, the next step is to be aware of whether or not those thoughts are limiting in some way.

How to do that? Simply ask yourself, 'In what way does thinking like this help me?' In any one situation ask yourself whether these thoughts are helping you or are shutting you down and limiting, blocking or restricting you or an aspect of your life in some way.

> **Try it now**
>
> Go back to Day 1. Look at the questions that you answered with a b) response. In what way do you think your b) responses are helpful? In what way are your b) responses unhelpful?
>
> For example, if for question 5 your response to the idea of learning a new skill was 'There's no point, it will take such a long time to learn and for me to be any good at it', ask yourself, in what way is that thought helping you? Is it opening up your world? Or is it limiting you? Is it closing you down and preventing you from coming up with any options, possibilities and solutions?

Acceptance and commitment

Being aware of the way you're thinking, and recognizing that it doesn't make you feel good or help you to get what you want, can prompt you to look at things from a different perspective. Once you're more aware of your limiting thoughts, you're in a better position to disempower them and to use them as a cue for positive action.

What you don't want to do, though, is to start arguing with yourself – telling yourself you are 'wrong' to think the way you do won't work. Neither will berating yourself – telling yourself that you 'shouldn't' be thinking like this. Instead, you simply move on to more positive, helpful thoughts.

In the practice of mindfulness, there's a concept known as 'acceptance and commitment' that can help you let go of the disempowering thoughts that are typical of a scarcity mindset and move on to more helpful, empowering thoughts that are typical of an abundance mindset.

An acceptance and commitment approach suggests that you acknowledge and *accept* a situation and your thoughts about it. You step back from your thoughts and then move on – you *commit* yourself – to more helpful ways of thinking, responding and behaving.

For example, if you were involved in a work project with colleagues who were not getting on and not working well together you might think, 'These people are a nightmare. This is never going to work out. Why did I have to be involved with this?'

You acknowledge and accept the situation and your thoughts about it. Maybe those colleagues *are* a nightmare and maybe the situation *won't* work out. Or maybe it will. Either way, railing about it and getting stuck in those thoughts is not helping you. You need to separate yourself from the negative thoughts.

Instead of getting caught up with your thoughts, notice them and let them go. Imagine, for example, a sheriff in an old Western town who notices an outlaw strolling down the main street. The sheriff acknowledges the outlaw and then calmly and firmly encourages him to keep walking, right on out of town. That's you, acknowledging those negative thoughts and then calmly telling them to keep moving along out of your mind. Instead of challenging your negative thoughts, you simply acknowledge and release them. If and when they come back, look them in the eye like that sheriff and tell them what they need to do: keep moving along.

Just as with the meditation, there's no need to analyse them or dwell on your thoughts. Instead, you notice the thoughts, recognize that they are not helping you in any way and you let them go so you can move on to more helpful ways of thinking, responding and behaving.

Exercise: Positive thinking

Turn back to the questionnaire in Day 1. Choose one of the questions and write it in your journal. As well as the positive a) response that's already there, think about what other, more positive thoughts *might* have been possible.

If you find this hard, think of yourself as a script writer. Imagine that you are simply writing alternative thoughts. You could also ask someone else for their ideas.

Now choose a couple more of the questions from Day 1. See if you can come up with more positive thoughts – thoughts that reflect options and possibilities.

If you change the way you think, you will create a change in how you feel, what you do and how you behave. So if we take the example of someone you know achieving or attaining something you'd like to achieve or attain, rather than think, 'That will never happen to me, I don't have the same skills/resources', you might think, 'I'm inspired! Maybe I could do that!' Thinking in this way prompts you to think of possibilities and options.

> **Try it now: Thought-changing prompts**
>
> When you notice that negative, limiting thoughts are starting to enter your mind, to prompt you to move on to more empowering thoughts, try one of these:
>
> - If you're sitting down, stand up.
> - If you're standing up, sit down.
> - If you're indoors, go to a different room.
> - If you're walking outside, change the direction you're walking.

Acceptance and commitment recognize that when you accept and let go of unhelpful limiting thoughts, you let go of the emotional aspects and allow the rational, logical part of your mind to start working for you, to think in more helpful, positive ways.

An acceptance and commitment approach emphasizes that no matter what you thought before, what matters is how you think from now on. In fact, just thinking about what you have to gain rather than what you have to lose will help you let go of limiting thoughts and commit yourself, your time and energy to positive thoughts and solutions.

Let your emotions alert you to the way you are thinking

In future, whenever you're feeling worried, disappointed, stressed, annoyed or upset, stop and become aware of your thoughts. It could be a travel delay, an event that got cancelled, something you lost or something that someone did or said that irritated you. What are your thoughts? Can you only see one way that events could turn out? Or are you aware of more than one option?

Exercise: The power of 'but'

A useful way to change negative, unhelpful thoughts into more helpful thoughts is to follow the negative thought with a 'but' and then complete the sentence.

'I don't think I can do this, **but** I'll try and if it looks like I can't manage, I'll ask for help.'

'I'm so unfit, **but** I can exercise and get fitter.'

Note how these sentences started out as negative thoughts. Now complete each of the following sentences to turn it into a positive thought.

- I'm so nervous about meeting these people, **but** ...
- I've let my friend down by cancelling our night out together, **but** ...
- I didn't get the job, **but** ...
- It's not fair, all my friends have better jobs than me, **but** ...
- I don't like living here, **but** ...

The word 'but' encourages you to complete a sentence with something positive. If you could just add a 'but' to every negative thought you produced, you could transform all negative thoughts into positive ones!

What's a limiting thought you've had that you can extend to a more positive sentence with the simple use of 'but'?

I _____, **but** _____

Any time you catch yourself saying a negative sentence, add the word 'but'. This prompts you to follow up with a positive sentence.

Exercise: 'And' not 'but'

How often do your thoughts start positively but end negatively? Look at these two sentences:

> I went for a run, **but** I only managed to get round the park twice.
>
> It's nice of them to invite me to dinner, **but** it was probably because someone else dropped out.

Here 'but' is a minimizing word that devalues the positive thought before it. Replacing the word 'but' with 'and' creates a much more positive meaning. By using the word 'and' you make it more likely that you will also come up with a solution – 'but' is final, 'and' implies there's still more to come.

> I went for a run **and** I managed to get round the park twice and tomorrow I'm going to try to do three times.
>
> It's nice of them to invite me to dinner **and** I'm looking forward to it.

In these examples, the word 'and' means the sentence ends in a positive way.

Key points

- A mindful meditation practice can help you be aware of the thoughts in your mind. Then, once you start being aware of your thoughts in everyday situations, the next step is to be aware of whether or not those thoughts are limiting in some way.
- In a variety of situations, ask yourself whether these thoughts are helping you or are shutting you down, limiting, blocking restricting you or an aspect of your life in some way.
- **Set yourself an intention:** Rather than get stuck in negative thoughts or difficult emotions, as soon as you are aware of them, let them be the cue to move on to more helpful, empowering thoughts.

Day 4

Moving away from comparing and competing

INTENTION

To focus on your own attributes and abilities – what you have done and are doing – rather than comparing and competing with others.

THOUGHT FOR TODAY

Comparison is the thief of joy.

Theodore Roosevelt

There's always someone you know, meet, see, listen to or read about who, one way or another, appears to have more than you: they may be more successful, more good looking, more capable, earn more or have done more than you.

Even if they haven't actually achieved more or got more, they may have something that you don't – the opportunity that you had hoped for, the job, the career, the house or the new partner you wanted.

Perhaps you read the social media posts of your friends, colleagues and people you don't even know, you see them going to glamorous events, having super holidays, having fun with their friends, and wonder why you're missing out. You compare your situation with theirs and find yours wanting; their strengths highlight your weaknesses. You doubt yourself, your abilities and your achievements.

Exercise: Not enough

Have you ever met, read or heard about someone else that left you feeling that you were not enough in some way? In your journal, write down any of these situations that you remember leaving you feeling that you were:

- not achieving enough
- not attractive enough
- not organized or tidy enough
- not disciplined enough
- not successful enough
- not clever enough
- not wealthy enough
- not deserving enough
- not _____ enough [fill in the blank!].

You can always find ways in which you don't match up – there's always a gap between yourself and someone else. Of course it's natural to want to know, compared to other people, how and where you fit in. But when we compare ourselves to others, we usually end up judging ourselves. Continually measuring what we haven't got and what we can't do with what other people have got and can do and concluding we don't match up can only lead to feeling inferior. You will end up disappointed with yourself and resentful of others.

A scarcity mindset

Once you start feeling 'less than', your reticular activating system (which you learned about on Day 2) prompts your mind to notice and pay attention to thoughts and beliefs that match what you already think and believe and have experienced. So when you feel 'less than' you may even look for further evidence to support and confirm what you've decided is true – the ways in which you don't match up, what you don't have, can't do or will never be. But thinking like this just serves to further encourage a scarcity mindset.

As well as thinking that you don't match up with others, a scarcity mindset believes that resources and opportunities are limited. With a scarcity mindset, you may believe that you *have* to compete with others – for jobs, places to live, friends, money, resources, access to education, better grades, access to health services and so on. A scarcity mindset also believes that if others get something, then you don't. There is only so much, and if someone else has it, that means there will be less for you.

With a scarcity mindset, you either compete with others or you just don't even try: you resign yourself to being unable to succeed in the same way that others do. In contrast, when you have an abundance mindset you believe that there *is* enough to go around. Rather than get stuck in envy or resentment you can be genuinely pleased for other people – for what they have, what they gain and achieve. In addition, you recognize that, yes, other people have achieved things that you haven't, but often, you see that as an inspiration, not a barrier.

Dragons' Den

An abundance mindset sees that although many good opportunities have already been acted on, there are also lots of opportunities out there that have not been thought of yet. We only have to watch episodes of the popular long-running TV series *Dragons' Den* – where entrepreneurs with an idea for a product or service pitch their business ideas to five multimillionaires who are willing to invest their own cash. Since the series started in 2015, there has been a continuous stream of entrepreneurs who enter with an idea for a service or product that, one way or another, is unique – no one else has thought of it. There is an abundance of new ideas.

Six steps to avoid the comparison trap

1. **Accept it.** If it's not possible to have what the other person has – their happy family life, their sporting ability or the fact that they're married to a rock star – accept it. Acceptance means recognizing when something is what it is and it cannot be changed. It means recognizing the futility of wanting something that you will never have or get.
2. **Know that you are good enough.** Whenever you are aware of yourself comparing, take a moment to remind yourself that you are good enough just as you are, even if you don't have something you see in others – for example, academic or career success, a beautiful home, celebrity social life or high-achieving children.
3. **Avoid social media posts.** Avoid the boasting and bragging of friends, colleagues and people you don't even know which, when you compare your situation to theirs, leaves you feeling envious, jealous, resentful or diminished in any way.
4. **Be inspired by others.** Rather than compare yourself with other people who are 'better' or have more than you, see others as role models to learn from and inspire you. When you open yourself up to feeling inspired by others, you are likely to feel motivated to achieve and do well according to your own abilities, skills and resources.

5. **Compare less. Appreciate more.** How often do you compare yourself with someone less fortunate and consider yourself blessed? That's not to suggest you compare yourself to others who are worse off than you to make yourself feel better. It's more about getting a sense of perspective. Be more aware of what you do have rather than what, compared to others, you don't have. Identify the good fortune, privileges and qualities you have and build on them. (We will look at this in more detail on Days 5 and 10.)

6. **Focus on you.** Comparing yourself to someone else puts the focus on the wrong person. Your skills, abilities, experiences and contributions and value are entirely unique to you. They can never be fairly compared to those of anyone else. Your time and effort could be better spent thinking positively about yourself. Compare yourself to yourself. Focus on what you have done and are doing rather than what everyone else has done and is doing. Reflect on what you've experienced, achieved and/or overcome. See how far you have come compared to last week, last year, two years ago, five years ago.

There is nothing noble about being superior to some other man. The true nobility is in being superior to your previous self.

Hindu proverb

Exercise: Identify what you have and have done

In what ways do you have more than before? In your journal write your answers to these questions:

- What do you know – what have you learned – that you didn't know a week ago?
- What can you do now that you couldn't have done one, two or three years ago?
- In the last year or two, what have you done for the first time?
- What new decisions have you made or what new actions have you taken that have resulted in you moving in a new, positive direction in your life?
- In the last year, what have you bought or acquired?

- What negative unhelpful behaviour or way of thinking have you freed yourself from?
- What positive behaviour or way of thinking have you introduced into your life?

Recognizing in what ways you have moved forward and gained is what counts. No matter how slowly, one way or another, you *have* moved forward and become more. When you are aware of that, you can stand taller as a result of the comparison instead of feeling diminished by it.

Every block of stone has a statue inside it and it is the task of the sculptor to discover it.

Michelangelo

It doesn't matter what anyone else is doing with *their* block of stone. The statue that they are creating is theirs. What you are doing with your own block of stone is what matters. That's why it's important to identify your own values, strengths and abilities, as you will see on Day 6 and Day 10.

Manage your envy

Envy can motivate and inspire you to improve your situation and to achieve your own goals, not just want what someone else has.

The next time you catch yourself resenting what someone else has and feel a sense of hurt combined with entitlement, recognize it for what it is – envy. Be aware that when envy narrows your mind, so that you're focused on what others have, you make it difficult to move forward in a positive way. You're stuck. Stuck in your envy.

Envy *does* have a positive purpose: to motivate you to achieve or attain whatever it is that the other person has that you want too. Use your envy to create a goal. If you want it, they probably did too. What might they have done to get what they wanted? Ask them. Rather than wallow in thoughts such as 'Why have they got it? It's not fair', change your focus. Start planning how you can work towards what it is they've got that you want. This will make you more positive and in control since you are no longer comparing what the other person has that you haven't – you'll be too busy working towards what you want. You won't have the time or a reason to be envious.

Shona's story

'When a new person – Lisa – joined our team at work, myself and my colleagues liked her from day one. As time went on she became a good friend but often, when I was around her, all I could see were my shortcomings staring back at me. She was everything I wasn't. Or everything I thought I wasn't – bright, funny, outgoing – and things always seemed to go right for her.

By comparison, everything in my life seemed less. I wasn't as fun. I wasn't as fearless. I didn't have as many friends. Everything I achieved somehow didn't measure up to her achievements. If I was being logical, I knew there were things that were good about me, but emotionally I sometimes felt overwhelmed with envy and resentment. She never said anything to make me feel this way, it was all me.

I considered myself a good friend, but when I talked to my brother about how I felt, he pointed out that I wasn't being a particularly good friend to myself. He told me, "You wouldn't be unkind enough to point out to someone else in what ways they don't match up and are less than another person. If you wouldn't say it to a friend, don't say it to yourself."

I realized that when I compared myself to her, I was only looking at her strengths and achievements and I ignored my own. My brother encouraged me to keep a record of all the good things I had done, to write what he called a "Ta Da! list".

It didn't matter how big or small, whatever it was that I achieved or attained, each evening I wrote down something. If I achieved something at work, if I helped a friend or anyone else. If I went for a run or to the gym on a morning I really didn't want to go, I wrote it down. Each week, looking at all I had achieved, both big and small, made me feel good about myself. I was much more confident. I was more aware of my own strengths, skills and qualities and I no longer saw Lisa as better than me. I could be pleased for Lisa's successes, as well as my own.

It's an ongoing practice. I continue adding to my "Ta Da! list". Regularly reminding myself has helped keep my confidence and self-esteem on an even keel.'

MAKE IT A HABIT: TA DA! LIST

Start a 'Ta Da! list'. No matter how big or small, whatever you have achieved or attained at the end of the day, write it down. At the end of the week, read through all the things you have achieved.

DAY 4

Key points

- You can always find ways in which you don't match up; there's always a gap between yourself and someone else. As well as thinking that you don't match up with others, a scarcity mindset believes that resources and opportunities are limited; that you either have to compete or you resign yourself to there not being enough for you too.
- In contrast, an abundance mindset believes that there *is* enough to go round. You can be genuinely pleased for other people, for what they have, what they have gained and achieved. In addition you can be inspired – if they've got it or done it, you probably can too.
- Compare yourself to yourself. Focus on what you have done and are doing rather than what everyone else has done and is doing.
- **Set yourself an intention:** Reflect on what you've experienced, achieved and/or overcome. See how far you have come compared to last week, last year, two years ago, five years ago. Talk to friends and family members. Ask them what they have achieved in the last few weeks, months or years.

Day 5

Abundance consciousness

INTENTION

To recognize and appreciate the abundance you already have in your life.

THOUGHT FOR TODAY

The moment we are content, we have enough. The problem is that we think the other way round; that we will be content only when we have enough.

Tibetan saying

What you believe is what you receive. Believe that there is plenty and there will be plenty. Believe that there is very little and you will receive very little. It can be easy to slip into 'I don't have enough' or 'I am not enough' thinking, to be dissatisfied and focus on what you haven't got or what's 'wrong' with your life. There is, though, a simple way to believe that there is plenty. It involves developing an 'abundance consciousness'. An abundance consciousness means being aware of, acknowledging and appreciating what is good and plentiful in your life right now.

If you focus on what is missing, it continues to be missing. But if you focus on what is present, it increases and intensifies – you start to see it and experience it everywhere: you have an abundance consciousness.

With gratitude you appreciate what you have. That doesn't mean that there's nothing to be done, that you can't have aspirations and aim for more. But gratitude is the foundation stone for abundance; an attitude of gratitude can shift you from a scarcity mindset to an abundance mindset. When you take time to appreciate all the ways in which life is good for you, scarcity disappears and abundance appears.

Exercise: Appreciate the things you already own

You can have all the money and possessions, friends, experiences and achievements that you wish for, but if you don't appreciate them, no matter how much you have or how much more you have, everything falls into a black hole – an abyss – of things you don't value, of things that you fail to appreciate and are not thankful for.

When it comes to your possessions, do you remember the initial thrill of buying any of them – new shoes, a new computer, a phone, a car or a fab new sofa? Most likely, by now, the excitement has worn off; you've got used to the things you've bought.

- **Write about it:** In your journal list three items you own. Describe in what way each item is useful to you or what it is about each item that you enjoy.
- **Talk about it.** Ask a friend or family member what three things they own that they appreciate. Ask them why those possessions are of value to them.

With an abundance mindset you are aware of and appreciate what you already have in your life. In contrast, with a scarcity mindset you believe you don't have enough and you want more. More love, more friends, more money, more possessions and experiences. But how can you ever have enough if you don't appreciate what you have?

Appreciate the things you already own; make a point of noticing and acknowledging the benefits and pleasures your things have brought you, so that your pleasure in them doesn't wear off.

Exercise: Train your reticular activating system (RAS)

Set a timer for five minutes. Now write down everything that you have achieved or enjoyed doing in your adult life. This will be easy to start with. Examples could include passing your driving test or a sporting achievement. Other examples could be related to your work or home, career, family and friends, health, sport, travel and holidays. After two or three minutes you will start to run out of things you've achieved. Don't stop though. Keep going and look for smaller achievements – things like decorating a room, decluttering your wardrobe or mending or fixing something. Spend all five minutes writing down everything you can think of.

The point of this exercise is to show you how once it knows what it's looking for, your reticular activating system will keep thinking of other things that you have achieved – that it's been prompted to notice – after the time is up. (More about this on Day 12.) You've primed your brain to be aware of the positive things in your life. You've created an 'abundance consciousness'.

Three more ways to increase your abundance consciousness

Hem your blessings with thankfulness so they don't unravel.
Author unknown

1. **Dwell on happy memories.** Look through the photos you took in the last year. Find between six and ten photos of happy occasions and events you've experienced. Get those photos printed at a shop or online photo printing service and place them somewhere in your home that you can see them. A year from now, do the same thing again.
2. **Appreciate the services you have received.** If you aren't aware that something has benefited you, you won't feel gratitude. So, the next time you pay a bill, think of something positive that the service or product has helped you achieve. This can shift your focus from thinking about what you had to give, to what you receive.
3. **Look for examples of abundance in nature.** It is the tendency of nature to produce more, and create more of everything. Look for an abundance of trees, plants. fruits and berries. Look out for fields of wild flowers in the summer. Step outside on a clear night and gaze at the infinite number of stars.

Habit to develop: appreciate three things

Think of three positive things that happened yesterday. Perhaps you had a good hair day. One of your favourite songs came on the radio. Or you ate a perfectly ripe avocado. It could be that the sun was shining or you enjoyed listening to the sound of the rain.

There's an abundance of small things that can make for positive moments. Managing to fix something – a cupboard door or a knot in a shoelace – are both things to be pleased about. So is dropping your phone and discovering that the screen was still intact. Or arriving late to meet someone only to find the other person was even later. Receiving a humorous text from a friend, your dog doing something that made you laugh or watching something good on TV. These are all examples of the small things that happen in any one day.

Keep a gratitude diary. From now on, at the end of each day, in your journal write down three good things that have happened that day. Even if you had a bad day, rather than dwelling on what went wrong, find three good things that happened. Get in the habit of noticing and reflecting what was good and right in your days.

You will soon find yourself actively looking for things to appreciate and, after a while, it will become second nature.

DID YOU KNOW?

Identifying the good things that happen every day is what people who pray do each evening when they thank God for the blessings of the day. You don't have to be religious to do this. You just need to make it something you do on a regular basis and know that not only can it help you feel good at the end of each day, but it contributes towards developing an abundance mindset.

Key points

- An abundance consciousness means being aware of, acknowledging and appreciating what is good and plentiful in your life right now.
- When you only tend to notice what you don't have in life, you will never have enough. In contrast, when you make yourself aware of and appreciate what you have in life, you will always have more.
- **Set yourself an intention:** Regularly remind yourself of what you have; what you have achieved, what you own and what you have experienced. Tell friends and family that you are doing this. Ask them to share with you, what they appreciate in their lives.

Day 6

Knowing your true self

INTENTION
To identify your values, to know what's important to you and is your true self.

THOUGHT FOR TODAY
Your values become your destiny.

Mahatma Gandhi

Now that you've taken the first steps away from a scarcity mindset towards an abundance mindset, you can move on to thinking about what it is in life that you would like more of – what you would like in abundance?

No doubt there are things you would like to attain and achieve. But how do you know if what you want are the 'right' things for the 'right' reasons? How, for example, can you be sure that what you want is right for you and not what you think you *ought* to have or *should* do. How can you be sure that it's what *you* want and not what other people think you should be pursuing? Perhaps, for example, as far as work and career are concerned, your family believe that qualifications, status and high earnings are important. But what if you don't share the same values, and right now, you would rather be selling ice cream on a beach in Spain? Or perhaps you aspire to be a tree surgeon rather than a heart surgeon? Or you want to be a tattoo artist, not a fine artist? Or you want to be a DJ, not a GP?

The best way to ensure you are aiming for what's right for you is knowing that your wants and wishes match your values.

We all have values and we each have different values. Maybe you've not given much thought to what your values are, but that doesn't mean you don't have them. Quite simply, your values are what's important to you and has some worth to you in the way that you live your life.

What have your values got to do with abundance? When you know what your values are – when you know what's important to you – you can be confident that what you want, hope and wish for is right for you; you know that you are being true to yourself.

Being true to yourself means living your life in ways that are in line with your values – doing what's important to you, not what you think you 'should' be doing, 'ought' to be doing or what other people think is important for you to have and to be. You are being your true self – you're being the real, genuine and authentic you.

Being true to yourself – living your life according to your values and according to what's important to you – isn't always easy. There are often difficulties, challenges and setbacks. Sometimes you may have to compromise on your values but ultimately, when you're being true to yourself, your aims and intentions reflect who and what you really want to be and to have.

Bronnie Ware spent several years working in palliative care in Australia, caring for patients in the last weeks of their lives. She talked with her patients and listened to them as they looked back over their lives. As a result of these conversations, in 2012, Bronnie published a book, *The Top Five Regrets of the Dying*. The top regret that people expressed? That they hadn't had the courage to 'live a life true to myself, not the life others expected of me'.

To live a life that's true to you, you first need to be clear about what your values are – what's meaningful and important to you.

Exercise: Identify your core values

To help you identify your values, here is a list of some common core values. Tick any that are important to you. Add any you think of that are not included on the list.

Achievement	Determination	Optimism
Adventure	Dignity	Peace
Affection	Directness	Perfection
Ambition	Duty	Persistence
Appreciation	Empathy	Popularity
Balance	Enjoyment	Privacy
Beauty	Equality	Punctuality
Belonging	Excellence	Reliability
Calmness	Excitement	Respect
Care	Fairness	Security
Certainty	Family	Self-control
Clarity	Fun	Self-reliance
Commitment	Generosity	Simplicity
Compassion	Gratitude	Sincerity
Confidence	Harmony	Spontaneity
Connection	Honesty	Stability
Contributing	Humility	Structure
Control	Independence	Success
Cooperation	Integrity	Support
Courage	Intimacy	Trust
Courtesy	Justice	Truth
Creativity	Kindness	Understanding
Curiosity	Loyalty	Unity
Decisiveness	Open-mindedness	Wealth

Once you've been through the list, narrow down your list to between five and seven values. These are your 'core' values – your most important, essential values.

Exercise: Interpret and better understand your values

Having identified your core values, give some thought to what each of those values means to you. Different values mean different things to different people so it's useful to define what each value means to you and how it relates to your life.

It's important to write it down. The process of explaining in writing what each value means to you can help you further clarify why it's important to you. For each value, answer these questions in your journal:

- What does the word (the value) mean to me? What does the dictionary say this word means? (Look it up on www.dictionary.com.) Do I agree with that definition? How would I describe to someone else what this word – this value – means to me, how it applies to my life?
- Why is this value important to me?
- In what way is this value currently a part of my life? How do I live this value? If, for example, kindness and compassion are values, how, where and when am I – or have I been – kind and compassionate?
- Do any or all of the values I've identified for myself also reflect what I want more of in my life? More stability, for example, or more privacy, kindness or fun?

Your values are a central part of who you are and who you want to be. Values can determine your priorities and help you to make decisions with confidence and clarity. If you act according to your values you can be sure you are acting with integrity. By becoming more aware of these important factors in your life, you can use them as a guide to point you in the right direction, to feel more confident that in a variety of situations, you are doing the right thing.

Six good reasons to know what your values are

1. Your values help to orient your life – they act as guiding principles for how to live your life.
2. Instead of allowing outside influences – friends, family, social media etc. – to shape your life, your values enable you to be true to yourself.
3. When what you hope to attain or achieve is in line with your values, you can be confident that you're aiming for the 'right' things.
4. Your values can help you to assess options and opportunities as they arise. They can help inform your decisions. You'll feel ok about turning down opportunities if they're not in line with your values, and you'll be able to confidently take advantage of opportunities that are in line with your values, knowing that they are right for you.
5. When you know what your values are, you're anchored in the power of your true self. You then have a secure foundation which is the basis for and helps support your wants, needs and wishes.
6. As you work towards achieving or attaining what it is that you want, you can know for sure what will constitute a win.

DID YOU KNOW?

If you look at the lives of people who have succeeded and done well in business, the arts, music, media etc., you will often see how their personal values have guided them, propelling them to the top of their fields. For example, Anita Roddick, founder of skincare and cosmetics company The Body Shop, espoused business values that were a reflection of her personal values. She harnessed her personal values of optimism, fun, caring, family and community to a business that grew from a single shop opening in Brighton in 1976 to hundreds of franchises throughout the world.

Key points

- Your values are what's important to you and has some worth to you in the way that you live your life.
- When you know what your values are – when you know what's important to you – you can be confident that what you want, hope and wish for – what you are aiming to achieve or attain – is right for you; you know that you are being true to yourself.
- **Set yourself an intention:** Identify your core values. Consider what each value means to you. Write them down and keep them somewhere as a reminder of your true self.

Day 7
What do you wish for?

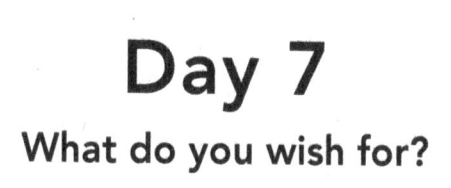

INTENTION
To identify what you would like to achieve or attain.

THOUGHT FOR TODAY
You are never too old to set another goal or to dream a new dream.
C.S. Lewis

As well as core values that relate to all areas of your life, you will have secondary values. Secondary values are what's important to you in the specific areas of your life. It's these secondary values that can help you be clear about what in your life you want more of or what you want to be bettered or improved upon.

Like many people, you may have a number of different areas in your life in which you might like to have more of something. Top of your list could be more money. Next might be more friends, or more travel or more free time. It could be that there's an aspect of your life where you would like things to be better or improved upon – your relationships with friends and family, your home life, your health or fitness, your job, your work, your studies or your career. Maybe it's to do with hobbies and interests, physical and cognitive abilities. Perhaps you'd like to develop or increase your skills and abilities in a particular area of your life.

What do you wish for?

It's helpful to think about the different areas of your life so that you can start writing down some ideas about what you would like to aim for. Over the next few pages are some suggestions.

FINANCES
If you're like most people, a large part of your interest in abundance concerns the possibility of financial abundance. You want to be rich! Wanting to be rich and wealthy is just as valid a reason to want more as anything else you want to achieve or attain.

WORK
If you work or you're aiming to work, you will have work values, beliefs about what's important to you – and what you wish for – in a job. What's important to you in your work or career? Here are some ideas to get you thinking:

- High earnings
- Flexible hours

- Travel
- Job security
- Responsibility
- Authority, leadership and influence
- Respect and appreciation
- Independence and autonomy
- Interesting, challenging work
- A variety of tasks and activities
- To start your own business or work freelance.

Is there something missing in your job, work or career – something that is important to you – around which you could create some work-related goals?

HEALTH

What's important to you when it comes to being in good health? If you are in good health, you might take it for granted and give it no thought or make no effort to maintain your good health. You might, though, want to set some goals related to your physical health, to be more fit and healthy.

It could be that you set goals related to your mental health; maybe, for example, you've been struggling with depression or anxiety and you want more peace and calm, to feel more balanced.

PERSONAL DEVELOPMENT

What do you wish for? Maybe you'd like to be more confident or assertive for example. You may want to develop your spirituality, if a strong sense of connection and belonging – of being part of something bigger, more eternal than yourself – is important to you.

FRIENDS AND FAMILY

What do you wish for? More friends? More connection, love and kindness in your life? What's important to you in a friendship and your relationships with family members? Perhaps having fun and lots of laughs together is what's important to you. Perhaps it's simply to have one or more shared interests. It could be that you are looking for mutual support, care and concern from friendships. It could be that you want to make more time to spend with your friends, family or partner. Just hang out together or do some fun, interesting things together; go to gigs, join a choir, learn a new skill together, maybe have a weekend away or a holiday together.

Are there friends you want to spend more time with? Have you even got the friends you want? Are you happy with the friends you have? Do you want more like-minded friends? Maybe you feel you have very few or no friends at all and you'd simply like to make some friends?

HOME
When it comes to where you live, what's important to you? What do you wish for? Is there somewhere you'd like to live – a particular place, house or home?

INTERESTS, HOBBIES AND SKILLS
Perhaps there's something you'd like to learn – something creative or practical or something that's simply fun. Would you like to play a musical instrument or learn a language? Maybe learning to sail, to ride a horse, to pick a lock or to master five magic tricks is something you would like to achieve?

Is there something you can already do that you'd like to get better at? Speaking another language for example, or playing the guitar or cooking? Perhaps being creative is important to you; you'd like to paint or draw, take photos, make pottery or design and sew your own clothes? Perhaps you want to travel and have more holidays? Visit Rome or Rio de Janeiro, Tahiti, Tibet or Turkey? Or go to see the Taj Mahal, hike along the Great Wall of China or the Grand Canyon?

Here are some more ideas to inspire you:

- Fly a light aircraft
- Dance the tango
- Play the guitar
- Hire a sports car

DAY 7

- Run a marathon
- Swim with dolphins
- Dye your hair blond
- Write a book
- Kayak through caves
- Milk a cow
- See the Northern Lights
- Go to Glastonbury Festival
- Eat in a Michelin-starred restaurant
- Ride a motorbike
- Sing, perform a drag act or do a stand-up comedy routine in front of an audience.

Exercise: Write a wish list

In your journal, write down anything and everything you would like more of. What matters to you? Write down anything you'd like to be better or improved upon in your life. Write down anything you can think of that you want to create in your life.

Don't worry about getting the list right. Just empty your mind; put down whatever comes up for you. Ideas can be realistic or unrealistic. Big or small. Mad or bad. But write them down.

Talk to others about it, ask them what they would include on their wish list. Share your ideas.

Top tip

Ask yourself what you would do if there was nothing to stop you – if you didn't have to think about money or other people in your life in order to achieve or attain whatever it is you are aiming for.

Being specific

In Lewis Carroll's *Alice in Wonderland*, Alice has the following conversation with the Cheshire Cat:

> *Alice*: Would you tell me, please, which way I ought to go from here?
> *Cheshire Cat*: That depends a good deal on where you want to get to.
> *Alice*: I don't much care where.
> *Cheshire Cat*: Then it doesn't much matter which way you go.
> *Alice*: ... So long as I get somewhere.
> *Cheshire Cat*: Oh, you're sure to do that, if only you walk long enough.

Once you've written your wish list, you need to narrow it down. If, like Alice, you don't know what, exactly, it is that you're trying to get to – what it is that you're trying to achieve, what you want more of or what you want to be improved in your life – you could well end up just about anywhere and spend a long time getting there!

You need to have one or more goals to aim for, and those goals need to be specific. If what you want more of is happiness, start by choosing a specific situation that you want to be happier in. If you want more money, is it a higher paid job you want? Your own business? Investments? Is your goal to travel more? How often? Where? When? Perhaps you want a better job? To do what? Do you want to work freelance? Or start your own business?

The more specific your goals are, the more likely you are to achieve them. Think about how much you want to achieve or attain and by when. Maybe you have a short-term goal – something you want to achieve in the next few days or weeks – or a longer-term goal – something you want to achieve in the next few months or years.

How to set goals you will achieve

Although working towards and achieving goals involves *doing* something, the way you think about goal-setting can make the difference between realizing your dreams and wishes or not. Three things will help: identifying the benefits, stating your goal in positive terms and sharing your goal with someone you admire and respect.

- **Identify the benefits.** Whatever it is, why is a particular goal important to you? In what way will you benefit from achieving your goal? Although to some extent you may feel your goal will be challenging, first and foremost your goal should inspire you. Identify the benefits, what you stand to gain from working towards and achieving each goal. Describe what you stand to gain in your journal.
- **State your goal as a positive statement.** Having aims and intentions and setting goals should inspire you and give you hope. Have you written your goal or goals in positive terms? With an abundance mindset, your intentions and goals are always stated in positive terms. Goals that are framed in such terms as 'stop,' 'lose' or 'quit' are limiting and are unlikely to motivate you. Instead of, for example, 'My goal is to stop smoking and lose weight', an abundance mindset phrases the intention in more positive terms: 'My goal is to become more fit and healthy and to look and feel better.' And instead of a goal that tells you what you don't want, such as 'My goal is to leave this job that I hate', an abundance mindset encourages you to identify what you *do* want: 'My goal is to get a job that I enjoy where I like the people I work with.'
  - **Goals framed in positive terms:**
    - tell you what to do rather than what not to do – you are more likely to achieve goals that get you what you want rather than goals that tell you not to do something
    - create positive energy and momentum instead of feelings of scarcity, deprivation and resentment
    - give you a positive path to follow – and the positive path generates positive thoughts which in turn encourages further positive action.

So, to increase your chances of achieving any goal, think of and write down a positive goal with a positive outcome. Your mind will be more willing to move towards a positive goal.

WHAT SCIENCE TELLS US

Tell someone you admire and respect: Research by Professor Howard Klein and his colleagues, at the Ohio State University's Fisher College of Business, found that people tend to be more committed to and achieve their goals after they share them with someone they see as being of higher social status than them, someone they look up to – whose opinions they respect. The study, which was published in the April 2020 edition of the *Journal of Applied Psychology*, found that when the study participants shared their target goal with someone they believed to be of a high status and whom they respected, they were more likely to reach their goal. On the flip side, those who relayed their goals to those of lower social status did not perform better. Similarly, the group who didn't tell their goal to anyone also didn't see any improvement in their motivation or successful achievement of their goal. The researchers suggest that sharing your goal with a 'higher-up' does more than keep you accountable, it also makes you more motivated, simply because you care what this person thinks of you.

Write down your goals: Having thought through what you would like to achieve or attain, do make sure you write down your goals so that you can actually see them. Don't let your ideas stay stuck in your head. If they are not written down, they are just dreams. Writing them down prompts you to define more clearly what your goals are. Writing them down also externalizes your ideas. Rather than trying to keep them in your head, writing down your goals frees up your mind to think about the next stage.

DAY 7

Key points

- You may have a number of different areas in your life in which you might like to have more of something. Start with a wish list and then narrow it down to a specific goal or number of specific goals.
- To increase your chances of achieving or attaining what it is that you want:
    - think about and write down your goals in **positive terms**
    - identify **when** you want to have reached your goal
    - identify the **benefits** – what you stand to gain from achieving or attaining your goal
    - talk about your goals – **tell someone** (a friend, a family member, a manager at work) whom you like and respect what you aim to achieve.
- **Set yourself an intention:** Identify and write down one thing (or you may have a number of things), no matter how small or big, that you can start working towards achieving or attaining, today.

Day 8
Visualizing what you wish for

INTENTION
To visualize working towards and achieving your goals and getting what you wish for.

THOUGHT FOR TODAY
The future you see is the future you get.

An effective way to encourage your reticular activating system to support you in working towards and achieving your goals is visualization.

More often than not, when you're planning to achieve something, you visualize it first. If, for example, you're planning a trip to a city in another country, you might see yourself going from your home by car, train or bus to the airport. Then you'd visualize the time you'll spend at the airport and then the flight. You'd then imagine yourself arriving at your destination and making your way to the car hire place. You'd then see yourself arriving in the city and making your way to your hotel.

This process of visualizing – of imagining and seeing – is useful to help you plan anything you want to do, to 'see' the steps and the final outcome. As well as alerting your brain – your reticular activating system – to be aware of resources and opportunities, it prompts you to be aware of any difficulties or problems you might have to deal with as you work towards what you hope to achieve or attain.

Furthermore, if you can imagine yourself achieving something, your brain then believes and accepts it is indeed possible and that you *can* do it. The future you see is the future you get. (If you constantly visualize *not* being able to do something, your brain believes and accepts that too.) Your brain can't tell the difference between having visualized making that journey to another country, for example, or having done it for real. This is because visualizing creates the neural pathways that your brain will use when it comes to doing something for real. And as you probably know, if you've done something successfully once, you're more likely to believe you can do it again. This is both reassuring and empowering, helping to build the confidence that is part of an abundance mindset.

DID YOU KNOW?

Visualization has long been something that top sports men and women have engaged in. Al Oerter, a four-time Olympic discus champion, and the tennis star Billie Jean King were among those using visualization in the 1960s. Heavyweight boxing champion Muhammad Ali used a number of mental practices including self-affirmation – proclaiming 'I am the greatest!' – and visualization to enhance his performance in the ring. He believed that if his mind could conceive it and his heart could believe it, then he could achieve it.

In more recent years, athletes of all sports routinely practise mental rehearsal: runners and rock climbers, swimmers and skaters, weightlifters, basketball and football players all now employ mental imagery to enhance their level of performance. For them, visualizing – or mental rehearsal – has become a multi-sensory endeavour. They use vivid, highly detailed internal images and run-throughs of the entire performance, engaging all their senses in their visualizing.

Exercise: Imagine past achievements

Think of a time when you achieved or attained something you'd hoped for. Picture what happened: the steps that led up to the achievement, what you did, where you were, who else was there. Then write about it. In your journal describe what happened and what you achieved.

Thinking about and visualizing what you have achieved and attained in the past can help you to feel positive and optimistic that you can do so again in a variety of other situations. The more you imagine yourself succeeding – even if it's something that happened in the past – the more likely it is to happen.

Creating new possibilities

You've probably watched natural history programmes and wildlife documentaries on TV. The sight of unusual plants and creatures, of the type you had never imagined before, completely changes your assumptions and broadens your ideas of what exists on our planet. Similarly, you can open up your own world by visualizing new possibilities. Creating images for yourself – pictures where you are achieving successful outcomes – will uncover new possibilities.

> **Try it now**
>
> Whatever you think is possible for yourself, when you expand your vision to reveal more possibilities and opportunities you are creating an abundance mindset. Not sure what that involves? Try this: look at a picture or photograph. Close your eyes and imagine what was in that picture. Then imagine what else could be in the picture. Now you are imagining new possibilities.

DID YOU KNOW?

When you visualize something, it can be from the perspective of yourself – seeing yourself through your own eyes or from the perspective of someone else. Seeing yourself through your own eyes is known as internal visualization. Visualizing yourself doing something from the perspective of someone else or as if you are watching a video of yourself is known as external visualization. Either method is an effective way to visualize.

'Outcome visualization' and 'process visualization'

There are two parts to visualization: 'outcome visualization' and 'process visualization'.

'Outcome visualization' involves imagining yourself reaching your goal: you create a detailed mental image of what it is you aim to achieve. If, for example, your aim is to run a marathon, you'd visualize yourself crossing the finish line, exhausted but exhilarated. You'd see your family and friends greeting you and congratulating you. You'd imagine all the excitement and the enormous sense of achievement.

The second, crucial part of visualization is 'process visualization'. It involves imagining each of the steps you'll take towards your goal. So if, again, it was a marathon, you'd visualize yourself starting off, running well, arms relaxed, breathing controlled. In your mind, with process visualization, you'd break the course into sections and visualize running each part, thinking about your pace, breathing and split time. You'd imagine what you'd do if you hit 'the wall', the point where your body and mind are simultaneously tested to the point of wanting to give up.

You may never run a marathon. However, you can use the same principles to achieve any goal by creating a strong image of yourself succeeding.

> ### Exercise: Outcome visualization
> Writing it down, or drawing a picture of yourself achieving your goal, is an effective way of visualizing. As you describe or draw what you will achieve or attain, you are automatically visualizing. Whether you want to start a business, hike in the Grand Canyon, play the trumpet or be a DJ, whatever it is, in your journal, write about or draw a picture of yourself doing or having whatever it is you hope to achieve. (On Day 11 we will look at visualizing the steps towards achieving your goals.)

Imagine how you will feel

Do more than just see yourself working towards and achieving what you are aiming for. Imagine, too, how you will feel – the emotions you might experience, such as pride and happiness. Recognize that you might also feel apprehensive, unsure or scared. That's ok. See yourself having courage, determination and resolve. These emotions are made up of positive thoughts, and create positive images that encourage you to move forward.

> ### Exercise: Create a vision board
> You may have goals to do with work or career, health and fitness, or financial goals. Perhaps you have goals to do with family and friends, or things you want to buy – clothes, equipment, furniture

etc – or hobbies or interests or fun things you want to do some day. Whatever your goals, a vision board – a collection of images and words that represent and reflect what you would like to achieve or attain – can help make your goals tangible and further remind you, encourage and inspire you.

Start by collecting images from magazines, postcards, leaflets, quotes and sayings and affirmations, the names of role models and anything you feel inspired by that represents any one specific goal that you are aiming to achieve. You'll need a big piece of cardboard, A3 or bigger, or a piece of flip chart paper. Stick the pictures and printed words in any order to create a collage. Make it a work in progress; keep adding images and words whenever you come across anything that relates to your goal.

You can also create a digital vision board. For example, Pinterest (pinterest.com) is one of the easiest ways to create a digital vision board. You can create boards for each and any specific goals. Google 'how to make a vision board on Pinterest'. Once you have created your online vision board, you can print it out at home or use a photo service to get a poster printed.

DAY 8

Key points

- An effective way to encourage your RAS to support you in working towards and achieving your goals is visualization. The future you see is the future you get. The more you imagine yourself succeeding, the more likely it is to happen.
- Creating images for yourself – pictures where you are achieving successful outcomes – will uncover new possibilities.
- **Set yourself an intention:** Regularly imagine yourself achieving your goal and getting what you wish for.

Day 9

Identifying your options

INTENTION

To identify your options – the possible ways you can achieve or attain what it is that you want.

THOUGHT FOR TODAY

Knowing you have options gives you the power of choice; you get to decide what way forward could work best for you.

Once you have identified what it is you wish for – more happiness, wealth, career success – and identified a specific outcome – whether it's to write a book that gets published, be picked for a part in a play, get a promotion or a pilot's licence – rather than release it into the 'universe of all possibilities' and hope to attract whatever it is that you want, you will need to put in time and effort to work towards achieving what you want. Today, we start by identifying your options – the possible ways you can achieve or attain what it is that you want.

Often, when a person has thought of something they want to have or to be, they assume that there's only one way of achieving it. But this approach reflects a scarcity mindset. A scarcity mindset limits your thoughts to what you know and what exists in your life right now. In contrast, an abundance mindset is aware that there's always new information, knowledge and possibilities. An abundance mindset recognizes that whatever it is you want to do – whether, for example, it's to live in the country and work from home or to open a restaurant in the city – more often than not, there's more than one way to achieve it. There are always options, possibilities and potential.

Exercise: Recognize possibilities

Three core hole bricks have three evenly spaced holes along their centre. Like all bricks, they are used for building walls, but there are many other possibilities. Google an image of a three core hole brick and then, in your journal, write down ten uses for a three core hole brick. Here are three ideas to get you started.

- A door stop
- A book end
- A candle holder.

Once you've run out of possibilities, ask other people for their ideas and add them to your list. See how many possibilities you can come up with.

DAY 9

A beginner's mind

Usually, what we do and how we think is based on what we think we already know. We tend to do things in the same way as we always have and we tend to think about ourselves, other people, objects, places and the world in the same way that we've always thought about them.

We make assumptions – beliefs that we presume to be true – about what is and isn't possible. It's your reticular activating system that's in control again – it works to ensure that your mind notices and pays attention to experiences that match its pre-existing thoughts and beliefs. It filters out everything that doesn't support your most prevalent thoughts. So first and foremost your mind notices and pay attention to thoughts, beliefs and experiences that match what you already assume and believe and have experienced.

But often our assumptions are based on outdated information or misinformation. Often, our assumptions are based on 'facts' that simply aren't true. Our assumptions then misguide us and limit our options and give us an excuse not to do something.

Responding to other people, situations and events in familiar, established ways limits how we receive and respond to the world around us. It makes it likely that we'll miss out on all sorts of possibilities and discoveries, new ideas and ways of seeing and understanding, solving problems and getting what we want. Is there a way around it? Yes, we can use a 'beginner's mind'.

A beginner's mind is a concept from the practice of mindfulness that suggests that everything can and does begin again, in the present moment. With a beginner's mind, you are aware that there's more than one way of thinking and behaving. With a beginner's mind you consciously put aside assumptions, beliefs, judgements and conclusions that are based on past ways of thinking and doing.

Four ways a beginner's mind encourages an abundance mindset

A beginner's mind helps you to:

1. **Let go.** You know that each time you let go of limiting thoughts that tell you there is only one way to think about something, you open yourself up to a number of possibilities.
2. **Be more aware.** Challenging your existing beliefs and considering new ideas can give you new perspectives, positive, fresh insights about what's possible for yourself, other people and the world around you.
3. **Be solution focused.** With a beginner's mind, rather than focus on problems and get stuck in difficulties, you focus on solutions and answers.
4. **Have new experiences.** Being open to fresh new ways of thinking about things can also open you up to new ideas, opportunities, experiences and ways of doing things, to begin again.

> ### Exercise: Identify your options
> An abundance mindset encourages you to think afresh about what is possible instead of what is not. You let go of your assumptions about what is and is not possible and move on to thinking of all the possible ways you could achieve your goal. Ideas can be realistic or unrealistic, it doesn't matter, because the important thing at this stage is simply to imagine all sorts of possibilities.
>
> However realistic or unrealistic, however big or small your ideas about the different ways you could achieve something, write them down in your journal.

Supposing, for example, you wanted to write a novel. Rather than resign yourself to not having the time to write, in order to find the time, you might see what your options are. For example, you could save up enough money to give up your full-time job for six months or a year, write in the day and do a bar job in the evenings and at weekends, or you could keep your job, get up early, write for an hour or two before you go to work and write in the evenings and at weekends, for maybe a year or two years.

You might have some goals related to your physical health. If your goal is that a year from now you'll be fitter and slimmer, then imagine all the ways that could happen. There may be several options. For example, you could join a gym – perhaps you could get a personal trainer or join with friends to hire a fitness trainer. Or follow online fitness classes? What type of exercise do you enjoy? Swimming? Cycling? Walking? Running? Would a 'Park Run' (parkrun.org.uk) be an option? If you need to lose weight, would joining a slimming club be helpful? Want to cut down on smoking or drinking? What are your options? What support is there for you to help you do that?

Zoë's story: a win–win situation

When Zoë was in her final year of university, she started making plans to travel in South America the following summer. Zoë loved socializing with her friends and meeting new people. She spent her days studying so the evenings were the only free time she had to see her friends. She thought through her options and realized that if she got a job for three evenings a week in a bar, she could see her friends and meet new people. She'd be earning money working behind the bar instead of paying to be in front of it!

The process of identifying your options will stretch you beyond your usual way of thinking and behaving. And because this positive approach opens up possibilities and ideas, you may well find that some of your ideas spark other ideas.

Exercise: Talk to other people

Think about how a friend or family member would go about approaching and achieving whatever it is you'd like to achieve. Then ask them for their ideas and insights.

You could also talk to others who have achieved what you want to achieve or attain. In your journal, write down three people you could ask. The three people might include someone you don't yet know, someone, for example, who is doing a job or has a career that you are interested in and you could approach for some advice and information.

Exercise: Assess your options

Once you've got some ideas and options written down, for each option, ask yourself some questions and in your journal, write down your answers.

- What skills, strengths and resources do I currently have that could be helpful for each option?
- What further information or knowledge do I need?
- Who could help – who could give me further advice, ideas or practical help?
- What are the pros and cons for each option?
- Which option appeals to me the most?

Be aware of how a particular option or idea makes you feel right now, when you think about it. Does it fit with your values? Or might you have to be flexible? If you feel positive and inspired, and feel it's a realistic, achievable way forward, then it's a good option.

Knowing you have options gives you the power of choice: you get to decide what way forward could work best for you.

Kit's story: doing the research

Kit was a trained nurse. He'd been working on an intensive care ward for the past five years. He was finding it increasingly stressful and thought about leave nursing altogether. Before doing so, he researched what other opportunities might be available. Kit discovered that amongst other roles, with some retraining, his options included being a children's nurse, a school nurse, a nurse in a care home, a health visitor or a midwife. But he also discovered that he could become a genetic counsellor – a role that up until now, he wasn't even aware was a profession. He applied for the role and the relevant training and successfully moved forward in a new direction.

Four top tips

1. **Write it down.** If you keep your ideas and options in your head, it's difficult to tap into more expansive thinking. There's only a certain amount of information your brain can hold before that information just clutters your mind. Writing down your thoughts and ideas not only empties your brain, it can also bring out more ideas.
2. **Take your time but not too much time!** Identifying and thinking through your options is a process that can't be rushed. It could take days or weeks to get all the information you need to make an informed choice.
3. **Make a well-informed decision, but know that the pursuit of more information can be a way of putting off a decision.** Trust your intuition. When you do feel strongly that a particular path or choice is the right one, know that it's because your decision is in line with your aims and values. Don't wait until conditions are perfect, get started now. If new information comes to light after you have decided which option to follow, if necessary, you can alter your course then.
4. **Accept uncertainty – make a choice despite possible unknowns.** Know there is no 'right' or 'wrong' option. When you're finding it difficult to make a decision, for each option, ask yourself, 'What's the worst that can happen? How might I deal with that?' Know that you *can* make a choice and if things don't work out you will already have thought of what to do to manage what happens.

Affirmations

You might find it useful to write down a positive affirmation and put it where you can easily see it, as a reminder that there are always possibilities, options and choices for how you go about achieving or attaining whatever it is that you wish for.

- There's *always* a choice.
- Knowing I have options gives me the power of choice.
- There's more than one way of thinking about a situation.
- There's no right or wrong choice. Once I've made a choice, I can *make* it the right choice.
- I take responsibility for my choices.

DAY 9

Key points

- A scarcity mindset assumes that there's only one way of achieving or attaining something. A scarcity mindset limits your thoughts to what you know and what exists in your life right now. In contrast, an abundance mindset is aware that there's always new information, ideas and knowledge that give you possibilities and options.
- With a beginner's mind you put aside assumptions, beliefs, judgements and conclusions that are based on past ways of thinking and doing. With a beginner's mind, you are aware that there's more than one way of thinking and doing.
- **Set yourself an intention:** Think about and write down the options you have for achieving or attaining any one specific goal that you have.

Day 10
Identifying your attributes

INTENTION

To identify the skills, strengths and abilities that will support you in achieving and attaining your goals.

THOUGHT FOR TODAY

Hide not your talents, they for use were made, What's a sundial in the shade?

Benjamin Franklin

Identifying your strengths

With an abundance mindset you focus on what you have, what you *can* do and what you're good at. You identify your attributes – your strengths and abilities – and think about how they can support you to work towards achieving and attaining the things you would like more of.

Your strengths are the personal qualities, abilities, knowledge and skills that you have. Strengths are things that at the very least, you are competent at – things that you have sufficient ability, knowledge and experience in. But more likely, your strengths are the things you're good at doing and good at being.

Exercise: Identify your qualities and strengths

Read through this list of attributes and, as you do, write down in your journal every quality that applies to you.

- **Adaptable and flexible**: I'm able to change my approach and adjust to different conditions and circumstances.
- **Adventurous**: I seek out and enjoy new and exciting situations and experiences.
- **Altruistic**: I'm concerned for the welfare of others – I'm happy to put aside my own concerns and welfare for the sake of others and do so without expecting any benefit for myself.
- **Open-minded**: I'm willing to consider new ideas and different ways of doing things.
- **Calm**: I can deal with problems as they happen; I don't get over excited or too anxious, angry or upset when things go wrong.
- **Conscientious**: I'm guided by a sense of what's right; I like to work carefully and do things thoroughly.
- **Confident**: I'm reasonably sure of myself – my beliefs, opinions and abilities.
- **Cooperative**: I work well with other people; I'm willing to be of assistance in working towards a common goal.
- **Creative**: I can think of new and productive ways of doing and achieving things.

- **Curious**: I'm eager to learn, to understand and know.
- **Decisive**: I make decisions easily, with little hesitation.
- **Determined**: I resolve to stick to a decision and/or keep going.
- **Empathetic**: I can easily understand and relate to what someone might be feeling in a particular situation, even if I have not experienced a similar situation.
- **Enthusiastic**: I have a lively interest in ideas, activities, tasks etc. I'm often eager to get on with things.
- **Honest**: I am sincere, truthful and genuine. I am honourable and fair in my intentions, what I do and say.
- **Independent**: I can easily think, act and do for myself – I'm not overly dependent on others or easily influenced by others' opinions or behaviour.
- **Intuitive**: I pick up on things easily – I often have an immediate instinct that tells me something is or isn't happening – that it is or isn't 'right'.
- **Imaginative, creative and innovative**: I can come up with new ways and ideas to make things happen and get things done and to solve problems and overcome difficulties.
- **Logical**: I'm capable of reasoning in a clear and consistent manner: I can easily work out what the next steps are.
- **Intuitive and perceptive**: I'm insightful, I know when something does or doesn't feel right. I can read between the lines, pick up on what others are feeling, what their needs, likes and dislikes are.
- **Methodical and organized**: I have clear methods and systems for doing things in an orderly way. I plan things efficiently.
- **Observant**: I'm quick to notice things. I notice details and I'm perceptive.
- **Optimistic**: I am usually hopeful and confident that things will turn out well.
- **Patient**: I can wait for things to happen in their own time. I can accept delay and difficulties without becoming annoyed or anxious.
- **Persistent**: I can continue a course of action in spite of difficulty or opposition. I can find a way through.

- **Practical**: I like to do whatever works, whatever is effective and brings results; I'm more concerned with the actual doing or use of something rather than with theory and ideas.
- **Reliable**: I can be trusted and depended on to keep my word, to do what I say I will, and to do something well.
- **Resourceful**: I'm able to find quick and clever ways to deal with new situations and overcome difficulties.
- **Resilient**: I can recover quickly from adversity, from difficulties and setbacks.
- **Responsible and accountable**: I can be trusted to do what I've said I'll do. I'm willing to ensure the job is done, and also accept responsibility for the results, whether they are good or bad. I don't make excuses or lay blame if something doesn't work out. I can explain, justify and take responsibility.
- **Sociable**: I enjoy being with and interacting with other people.
- **Sympathetic**: If someone is struggling or suffering in some way, I care and can be supportive.
- **Tactful**: I'm good at dealing with difficult or delicate situations; I know what to say or do to avoid giving offence.
- **Meticulous and thorough**: I take care to do something carefully and completely. I take care to perfect the details.
- **Tolerant**: I can put up with difficult situations and people.

Add to your list any other qualities or strengths you have. Then decide which of the qualities you have identified, are your five strongest qualities. Write them down in your journal.

Exercise: Past achievements and successes

Now, for each of those five qualities, think about how each quality has helped you in the past to achieve or attain something that you wanted to have or do. Write about it in your journal.

For example, if you felt that patience and persistence were two of your qualities, you might recognize that when you have had to work on something for a long time, your ability to calmly and steadily persevere paid off; you eventually achieved what you were aiming for. If being imaginative and innovative are two of your strengths, you'll know that you can come up with new ways and ideas to make things happen and get things done. Can you think of times in the past when you've done that? And if you're cooperative, you work well with other people. How, do you think, that has helped you achieve something?

Whatever it is that your qualities and strengths have helped you achieve in the past – they can do so again.

DID YOU KNOW?

In Buddhism, 'dharma' refers to the essential quality or character of something. It is a concept that encourages a person to recognize and act in harmony with their own nature, with their own unique values, qualities, strengths and abilities. It then follows that living your life in harmony with your true nature will result in you living according to your true purpose in life.

Deepak Chopra, the Indian-American speaker and author on the subject of the mind/body connection, suggests a concept he has named 'The Law of Dharma'. The Law of Dharma posits that when we use our unique gifts or special talents for the service of others, 'we experience the ecstasy and exultation of our own spirit, which is the ultimate goal'. You can learn more about sharing your attributes on Day 15.

Identifying your skills

As well as personal qualities and strengths, you will have skills. Skills are the abilities you have that have come about either as a result of a natural ability or talent you have or as a result of you learning and/or practising something.

Think of the skills you have – those that you've acquired through work, study, hobbies and interests. Perhaps you have good research skills – you're good at finding relevant facts and information? Maybe you have good IT skills? Perhaps you have good analytical skills? Do you have any specific practical skills? Maybe you have creative skills and abilities – you can draw, sew, create and make things?

> ### Exercise: Identify your skills
>
> In your journal, write down any skills that you have. Ask yourself questions to help you to write about your qualities and skills:
>
> - How has this skill helped me in my work or day-to-day life? What have I achieved or attained with any of my skills or talents? It may be that a particular skill or talent – drawing and illustrating for example – has enabled you to have a career and earn a living. Maybe you are good at learning, understanding and speaking a foreign language? In what ways has that benefitted you?
> - What challenges have I overcome by having this quality or skill?
>
> Whatever your strengths, skills and abilities, once you know what they are, you can think about how those abilities and qualities might help you achieve and attain whatever it is you are aiming for. So, ask yourself: what strengths, skills and abilities do I have that could contribute to me getting what I want?

Using skills and strengths to achieve a goal

Jo needed to increase her income in order to pay off some debts and then start regularly putting money into a savings account. She considered her options and decided to devote three evenings a week to doing something that would earn her the money she needed. Jo enjoyed watercolour painting; she looked at websites, such as Etsy, that sold handmade crafts online to see what sold well. Jo decided to paint watercolour pictures of animals. As well as her artistic skills, Jo's strengths were that she found it easy to focus, she was disciplined and determined. Using her skill as an artist and her strengths, Jo made a success of her sideline and she achieved her goal of paying off her debts and starting a savings account.

People with an abundant mindset know their skills, strengths and qualities and they set things up to succeed according to their attributes. You can do the same!

Affirmations

By identifying your skills, strengths and abilities, and writing out how, why and when you have each quality, you are creating your own personal affirmations – positive truths about yourself.

With a scarcity mindset typical thoughts are, 'I'm no good at this' or, 'I'll never get what I want' or, 'It's not fair, other people always do better than me'. These are negative affirmations – negative thoughts that we have about ourselves. Often, we continue to repeat these negative affirmations and in so doing, establish beliefs about ourselves that are limiting and serve to shut us down and prevent us from achieving and attaining more from life.

If, however, we create positive affirmations about ourselves and repeat them often enough, we will also believe them to be true. Positive affirmations help you to develop and maintain an abundance mindset; they enable you to feel confident and empowered. Positive affirmations contribute towards you getting what you want.

The affirmations that are going to most effective and beneficial are the affirmations that resonate with you the most – that you can believe to be true about yourself. You might, therefore, choose the sentences that describe your strengths. For example, if being conscientious was one of your strengths, your affirmation might be, 'I'm conscientious; I'm guided by a sense of what's right; I work carefully and do things thoroughly.' And if one of your strengths was honesty, your affirmation might be, 'I am honest; I am sincere, truthful and genuine. I am honourable and fair in my intentions, what I do and say.'

Exercise: Create personal affirmations

Choose one or more of the affirmations below or make up your own. Simple affirmations work best because they get right to the point and they're easy to remember. Then, with each affirmation you have chosen, today, in your journal, write it out three times.

You could also write one or more of these affirmations on a sticky note that you put somewhere you can easily see it. Each time you read the words, pause for a few seconds and consider the truth of each affirmation.

- When I act according to my true nature, I experience true being.
- No one is me and that is my power.
- The truth of who I am and what I am capable of moves me forward.

Regularly check in with yourself using a positive affirmation to remind you of your attributes and what you are capable of.

DAY 10

Key points

- Whatever your intentions, your aims and aspirations, dreams and wishes, they will come about as a result of your efforts and your abilities.
- Consider how your attributes – your skills, strengths and abilities – can help you achieve and attain the things you want.
- **Set yourself an intention:** Choose one of your top five strengths or skills. Think of a way you can use that skill or strength one time over the next few days.

Day 11
Getting what you wish for, one step at a time

INTENTION

To plan and carry out the series of steps you will take to achieve your goal.

THOUGHT FOR TODAY

The man who moves a mountain begins by carrying small stones.
Chinese proverb

Dream it, think it, plan it, then do it

Once you're clear about what it is you want to achieve or attain and you've identified your options and decided which option to take, the next thing to do is to take action. The most effective approach is to break things down into small, doable steps and to move forward one step at a time.

Exercise: Past achievements

In your journal, write down any of the situations from the list below that you've achieved:

- Had a holiday or a short break
- Learned to drive
- Moved into a new home
- Got the job
- Got the place on a course
- Completed a charity challenge
- Decorated a room
- Cleaned the bathroom.

Add to your list any other goals you set yourself in the past and subsequently achieved.

Next, choose one of the goals that you achieved. Can you remember the very first thing you did – the first step you took? And the next? And the next? And after that?

In your journal, write down each step you took. To do this, it might help you to write out the steps as if you were advising someone else – giving them a set of instructions on how to do whatever it was that you did and achieved.

Achievement _____
Step 1 _____
Step 2 _____
Step 3 _____

And so on; continue with as many steps as you need.

DAY 11

The benefits of a step-by-step approach

Any goal – anything you've achieved or attained – has been as a result of a series of steps that you have taken. What could feel impossible in one giant leap becomes a lot more doable as a series of smaller steps. Taking a step-by-step approach is the most positive way forward because:

- It makes achieving the goal more manageable. You avoid feeling overwhelmed.
- It's easier to get straight on to the next step if you've already planned what and how you are going to do it. It allows you to maintain a steady pace and keep the pace going.
- You remain focused on what you're aiming for. When you are taking regular consistent action, you are also regularly thinking about what you are doing and what you want. Your reticular activating system will act on this and alert you to new opportunities that will further help you to success.
- You set yourself up for constant successes by achieving small targets along the way.
- Each time you achieve a small part of your goal, you will feel a sense of achievement, and see yourself getting closer to what you want.
- Doing things one step at a time also gives you time to look at what is working and what isn't, and to decide if you need to change tactics.

Exercise: Identify and plan the steps

Whatever it is you are hoping to achieve or attain, start by writing down all the things you think you'd need to do towards your goal. You don't need to write things down in any particular order just yet. Just empty your mind, then write down everything you can think of that will need to be done.

Next, you will need to plan the tasks – the steps you need to take – and think through how and when you'll do them. Make a written list, outlining your steps. Ask yourself what you are going to do first. What will be the next step after that? And the one after that? And so on. And with each step, see yourself – visualize yourself – doing it.

Visualizing

On Day 8 you read that with visualization, there are two parts: 'outcome visualization' and 'process visualization'. 'Outcome visualization' involves seeing yourself reaching your goal: you create a detailed mental image of what it is you aim to achieve.

The second, crucial part of visualization is 'process visualization'. It involves imagining each of the steps you'll take towards your goal. So, if you were planning to run a marathon, you'd visualize yourself starting off, running well, arms relaxed, breathing controlled. In your mind, with process visualization, you'd break the course into sections and visualize running each part, thinking about your pace, breathing and timing. You'd imagine what you'd do if you hit 'the wall' – the point where your body and mind are simultaneously tested to the point of wanting to give up – and how you would manage that.

You may never run a marathon. However, you can use the same principles to achieve any goal: picture what you will be doing during each step towards your goal. In fact, as you think through each step, you automatically visualize – see yourself – carrying out each step. Be aware of this – as you think through and write out each step, be aware of yourself visualizing.

Plan for difficulties

Do anticipate potential problems and possible solutions. For each step, think about what could go wrong. What's the worst that could happen? What might the potential problems be? Think how you could deal with that. Who could help? What support, advice, or resources could you draw on?

Asking yourself questions like this is not to discourage you and put you off doing what you want to do. On the contrary, it's making it more likely you'll be successful because you've anticipated the potential problems and you've already thought through how you might deal with them.

DAY 11

Take action

He who thinks too much about every step he takes will always stay on one leg.

Chinese proverb

Having written a list outlining your steps, decide what is the one thing you'll do first. Don't overthink it. The more you think about whether you should or shouldn't do something, the less likely you are to take that first step. Once you've decided to do something, don't wait, do it!

Make the first step as easy as possible. Do that one thing, take that first step. Once you start doing something, it's easier to continue doing it. When you've completed that step move onto the next step. And then the next one.

Depending on what each step involves, you may be engaged with more than one step at a time. For example, if you want to be more fit and healthy, you might be working on exercising *and* eating more healthily at the same time.

Four top tips

1. Any one step may be challenging in some way. If it feels overwhelming or too difficult, break that step down into a few smaller steps.
2. Even with the steps that you find challenging, be aware that every task you complete brings you closer to the ultimate goal.
3. Don't get too caught up with and stressed by deadlines. Instead, focus on working consistently towards what it is you want to achieve, one step at a time.
4. As you complete each step, review the outcome. What's worked? What helped and went well? What hasn't worked? What needs adjusting? Write about it in your journal.

Leo's story

Identifying goals and options and taking it one step at a time is the approach that helped Leo Babauta to get out of debt. In his blog (zenhabits.net) Leo explains that it all started with his goal to quit smoking, a goal he attributes to setting a chain of other positive changes in motion. In his blog, Leo writes: 'Quitting smoking taught me a lot about changing habits and accomplishing goals, and all the elements needed to make this successful. I had tried and failed to quit smoking before, and when I was successful this time, I analysed it and learned from it and was inspired by my success. Success can breed success, if you take advantage of it.'

Leo says that in order to relieve stress without smoking, he took up running. He started out by running about half a mile and slowly built up his distance and within a month was running his first 5K. Very soon, he was so into running that he decided to run his first marathon.

In order to fit running into his day, Leo decided to start waking early. And once he started doing that he discovered the joys of the quiet morning hours. He realized that he got so much more done in the morning, not work, but working on his goals.

Leo was able to achieve another of his goals – to pay off his debts in a little over two years while supporting his wife and family of six children. He explains in his blog that he stopped living from one pay cheque to another, that he learned how to stick to his budget, spend less, save and pay off debts. He started with some smaller bills and in a year managed to pay off every one of his debts. 'It was amazing!' writes Leo. 'I now live debt-free.'

Leo has since gone on to create the website Zen Habits. You can read more about how he did this at: www.zenhabits.net/my-story/

Be flexible

Whatever you want to do and however you choose to go about it, your plans don't need to be fixed. As you work towards whatever it is that you want to achieve, you may need to adjust the steps you intend to take as you go along. New ideas may come up. As might difficulties and problems. Be prepared to change course in light of the unexpected.

DAY 11

This doesn't mean that you give up on a great idea. It means that you're not limiting your chance of success by focusing on just one way to accomplish it.

It can be helpful to have a plan B, an option that you can implement if the original one proves impractical or unsuccessful. In fact, when you were considering your options – the ways you could achieve or attain what you were hoping for – you will have already identified a plan B. And a plan C and maybe even a plan D!

As the saying goes, if Plan A doesn't work, the alphabet has 25 more letters.

Key points

- Any goal – anything you achieve or attain – will be the result of a series of steps. What could feel impossible in one giant leap becomes a lot more doable as a series of smaller steps.
- You will need to plan the steps you need to take. Anticipate and plan how to manage potential difficulties. Visualize yourself taking each step. Then get started!
- **Set yourself an intention:** Make the first step as easy as possible. Do that one thing, take that first step. When you've completed that step move onto the next step. And then the next one. And so on.

Day 12
Manifesting what you wish for

INTENTION
To understand how the unique power of mind can help you achieve your goals.

THOUGHT FOR TODAY
You always see what you are already looking for.

You may have come across the concepts of the 'law of attraction' and 'manifesting'. Both these concepts suggest that by simply placing your attention and focusing your thoughts on what you want to achieve and attain in your life – love, wealth, happiness etc – you will energize whatever it is that you desire and draw it to you – attract it or 'manifest' it into your life.

According to the law of attraction, as long as you have clarified your wishes – you have a specific goal – you just need to surrender it to the universe and let the universe manifest whatever it is that you wish for.

The law of attraction claims that every positive or negative event that happens to you is 'attracted' by you and your thoughts and your ability to send your wishes and desires out to the universe.

Do you want more friends? Perhaps you want to run a successful business or work in a job you love? Want to travel the world? The law of attraction suggests that you can attract these things. Want the perfect partner? You can attract – or manifest – that too simply by sending positive thoughts out to the universe.

Conversely, if something has gone wrong in your life – if, for example, someone has treated you badly – you will have attracted that as well. That's because the law of attraction brings to each person the conditions and experiences that they predominantly think about or expect.

With the law of attraction, there are three basic steps: ask, believe and receive. Ask the universe for it. Identify something you want or need in your life and then simply place the order with the cosmos by asking for it. The universe will answer. Think positively and see – or visualize – what you want as *already* yours. You'll need to know exactly what it is that you want. If you're not clear the universe will get an unclear frequency and will send you unwanted results.

Exercise: The car park

Imagine that you have driven into a large car park and you are looking for a space to park. Do you notice all the red cars or all the spaces?

A short while later, you return to the car park. You're looking for your car. It's a red car. Are you likely to notice all the car parking spaces or the red cars?

> If you found a parking space in a packed car park, the law of attraction would claim that you had 'attracted' that parking space from putting it out to the universe and as a result of your positive expectation that a space would be there, waiting for you. It would also suggest that when you returned to the car park you quickly found your red car because you asked the universe to find it for you.

Your amazing brain

The truth is, you found both the space and your red car as a result of the workings of your *brain*. On Day 2 you will have read how, for the sake of speed and ease, the reticular activating system in your brain works to ensure that your mind notices and pays attention to experiences that match its pre-existing thoughts and beliefs. It filters out everything that doesn't support your most prevalent thoughts.

When you drove into the car park, you were thinking about finding a parking space. So your brain and your vision were already on high alert for noticing a parking space, not a red car. But when you returned to the car park, your brain and all your senses were primed to notice a red car, not a parking space. There's nothing magical or cosmic about it; your mind simply notices and pays attention to what it's hoping and expecting to find.

DID YOU KNOW?

Web browsers and websites use algorithms which register your preferences and likes and give you more of what you have been looking at and are interested in. Your brain does the same.

We see what we are looking for

You may have noticed that once you are aware of something, you see it or hear about it everywhere. Think about taking a trip to Europe by train or going on a cruise for example, and you will be much more conscious of articles, travel programmes on TV and adverts for train travel and cruises. You will also be more likely to tune in when you overhear other people talking about train travel and cruises and the places you hope to visit. In another example, if you need to buy a new front door you'll suddenly be aware of every front door that you pass! Whatever becomes of interest or a priority to you, your RAS will direct your attention to be aware of more of it or anything that is relevant to it.

Furthermore, your brain is continually looking to prove you right and to confirm your thoughts and your beliefs, whether those beliefs and intentions are positive or negative. If you feel nervous about going to a party, for example, your brain will look for evidence that you are right to be anxious or nervous. You get what you expect because your RAS alerts you to what you already think, believe or know.

Exercise: The house

As you read this story, write down anything you think might be of interest to an estate agent.

'Mum works all day on a Thursday so today is a good day for bunking off lessons,' said Al to his friend Josh. 'Let's go!' The two boys ran until they got to the driveway of the house. Tall hedges hid the house from the road – the boys slowed down and strolled across the large pretty front garden. 'I didn't know your house was this big,' said Josh. 'Yes, but it's nicer now since we had a conservatory built and a new stone fireplace put in.'

There were front and back doors and a side door that led to the garage, which was empty except for three mountain bikes. They went into the house through the side door. Al explained that it was unlocked in case his younger sisters got home before their mum. Josh wanted to see the house. Al started in the living room which had recently been re-decorated. Al put some music on and turned up the volume on the new sound system his parents had recently bought. 'Someone will hear us!' said Josh. 'No they won't,' said Al. 'The nearest neighbours are a quarter of a mile away.'

The formal dining room with all the bone china, silver and cut glass was no place to play, and anyway the boys were hungry. They went into the big, bright kitchen and raided the fridge for something to eat.

Al said they wouldn't bother going to the basement – it was damp and had a musty smell. Instead he took Josh to his dad's study. 'This is where Dad keeps his signed photos of rock stars – Madonna, David Bowie, The Beatles – and his rare coin collection,' said Al.

There were four bedrooms upstairs. Al showed Josh his mum's en suite dressing room with its designer clothes and the locked box which held her jewellery. Then Al showed Josh his own room and pointed out the leak in the corner of the ceiling where the old roof had rotted. Finally they went into Al's big brother's room where they played on the games console for the next hour.

Now reread the story and write down anything you think might be of interest to a burglar. Notice how what is of interest to the burglar is different from or for a different reason than what is of interest to the estate agent.

Five more examples of your RAS in action

Hopefully, it's now clear how your RAS works for you – that at any one time, it alerts you to what is of interest or important to you. Here are five more examples:

1. You learn a new word, and that word appears to pop up all the time.
2. In a crowded room, you hear your own name being mentioned above the noise of everyone talking. And you can hear your own child's voice or cry over and above other children's voices or cries.

3. Someone says something, gives you some information or advice and you have an 'a-ha' moment because right then, it is relevant to what you needed to know. You might have heard the same advice before, but it's only now that it is important, so you pick it up.
4. You're driving your car. You are alert to cyclists, speed limits and speed cameras. You don't notice these things when you are walking.
5. You are scared of dogs. Out in public you can spot a dog a mile off.

The RAS helps keep us safe – to recognize danger – and to enable us to succeed in specific situations. It's context-based and filters out unnecessary phenomena to allow us to be aware of what, at the time, is important for us to avoid or achieve and attain.

Although your RAS usually works at a subconscious level – without you being aware of it working – the marvellous thing is that you can also *consciously* use it to alert you to anything – information, advice, ideas, opportunities and resources – that will help you to achieve or attain what you want.

Taking advantage of your RAS

Once you have identified what you want to achieve or attain, you can take advantage of your RAS by consciously using it to alert you to any relevant ideas and opportunities, information or resources that will support you in achieving or attaining what you are aiming for.

Whether you want a particular breed of dog as a pet, to spend the weekend at Glastonbury music festival, or to live and work in another country, whatever it is that you want, once you're clear about what specifically you want, you'll be more likely to tune in to the relevant information that helps you achieve or attain it.

If you're not clear about what you want, you miss out on opportunities as your RAS has nothing to go on. This is why it is so important to be clear about what you want to achieve or attain. If you think in general terms – that you just want to be rich or to be happy – your RAS doesn't know what it is exactly that will go towards making you rich or happy. So it doesn't know what to look for and alert you to. You need to be specific about what you want. This will get your reticular activating system working for you.

You don't have to put out a request to the universe and hope that by doing so, you will attract what you want. But you do have to be clear about what you want and be alert, aware and ready to receive ideas, information and opportunities that can help you move closer to achieving your goals.

Your intuition can help you. Intuition is that keen and quick insight, that immediate knowing that alerts you to something that is or isn't right. Everyone has intuition; it bridges the gap between the conscious and non-conscious parts of your mind, between instinct and reason.

Exercise: Tune in to your intuition

Intuitive messages are keen and quick and are often are missed because of all the other internal and external noise and activity that is going on in and around you. You can, though, practise developing your intuition, to be alert and aware of what's happening both within you and outside of you.

- Take a couple of minutes to be still and be present in a range of situations at home, on your way to work, at work, in a café, and so on. Breathe normally. What do you see or hear?
- Go outside or look out the window. Notice what is new or different, the changing light, sights, sounds.
- Notice what's normal *and* what's new or different in familiar situations. When you notice things being out of place or unusual you know you are being alert and aware.

Magical thinking – a benevolent power

At the beginning of this day – Day 12 – you will have read about the 'law of attraction'. You will have read that it's not, as the law of attraction suggests, the cosmos that brings to your attention what you need to help you get what you want. It's the workings of your brain – your RAS – that alert you to the opportunities, information, people or resources that will support you in achieving or attaining what you want and wish for.

The law of attraction and the concept of manifesting are examples of magical thinking. Like superstition, magical thinking is the belief that seemingly unrelated events are causally connected despite there being no real plausible link between them.

You might wonder why then, if the belief that you can attract or manifest what you desire is an irrational belief, so many people put stock in such beliefs, especially if they know there's no logical basis for them. The answer is that the beliefs can be beneficial even if they don't actually appear to have power.

There is a spiritual aspect to magical thinking. Spirituality is concerned with the experience of feeling connected to something in life that is more eternal or larger than yourself and moves, impresses or inspires you (more on spirituality on Day 19). Just as spirituality provides a sense of connection, so can magical thinking. Magical thinking can provide a sense of connection to a benevolent power, a power that's characterized by or expresses goodwill and kindness.

The belief that a benevolent power – although unexplained and irrational – can help you is, as the musician Nick Cave discovered, a source of hope, comfort and support. In an interview published in the *Observer* newspaper on 11 September 2022, he described the way that, after experiencing a bereavement, he found himself embracing 'a kind of magical thinking' instead of his more rational impulses, and noted how comforting and necessary such an approach was, and how it persisted.

As well as providing a sense of connection to a benevolent power, having faith in the law of attraction and manifesting can be seen as a form of positive thinking – being optimistic, open to possibilities and believing the best can happen. And that's a good thing!

DAY 12

Key points

- Whatever becomes of interest or a priority to you, your reticular activating system will direct your attention to be aware of more of it or anything that is relevant to it.
- Once you have identified what, specifically, you want to achieve or attain, you can take advantage of your RAS by consciously using it to alert you to any relevant ideas and opportunities, information or resources that will support you in achieving or attaining what you are aiming for.
- **Set yourself an intention:** Practise becoming more aware and tuning in to your intuition.

Day 13
Getting started and staying motivated

INTENTION

To move past any reluctance to get started; to get going and stay motivated.

THOUGHT FOR TODAY

> Twenty years from now you will be more disappointed by the things that you didn't do than by the ones you did do. So throw off the bowlines. Sail away from the safe harbour. Catch the trade winds in your sails. Explore. Dream. Discover.
>
> Mark Twain

Do you have a long-held dream? Is there something that you have wanted to do, something you've wanted to achieve or attain for some time but for whatever reason, you haven't done it? It may not be your life purpose, or even life changing, but whether it's big or small, what, if anything, have you done to make your dream come true? You can ignore the dream and choose not to follow through on it. But one way or another, as a dream often does, it will come back to you again and again.

Are you waiting for something or someone in your life to change before you take action? Maybe you think you don't know enough, or haven't done enough, you aren't confident enough, prepared or secure enough to move forward with what you want to achieve or do?

Exercise: What's stopping you?

In your journal, write down something that for some time now, you've wanted to do, but haven't yet done it. Then write down which of the following reasons has stopped you from getting started:

- I'm not ready.
- It's not the right time.
- It's going to be too hard.
- It will take too long.
- Maybe I'm not meant to do it.
- I'm too old/too young.
- It's too late.
- I don't have enough money/time/experience.
- I don't have the energy or the commitment.
- I might not do it right.
- What if I fail? I hate to fail so much that I'd rather not try just in case I fail. That way, I'll never fail at anything, because I won't try anything.
- Other people in my life won't approve or like what I'm doing.
- Most people don't succeed at what I want to do, so it's unlikely that I will either.
- I'm not good enough.
- I'll start tomorrow/next week/next year.

These reasons for not doing something can often sound quite convincing. They are characteristic of a scarcity mindset. If you believe them and you stay in your comfort zone, nothing will change and you won't get more of what you want in life.

Whatever you want to do or achieve, there will always be something you could point to that's standing in your way, or something you need to do before you can fully commit yourself. You can sit around and dream, make plans and wait for everything to be just right, but nothing is ever going to happen until you actually start getting on with it.

Perhaps you tell yourself that you'll get to it later. But if not now, then when? Don't wait for a time in the future when you'll have the time, the money, or whatever it is you think you need first.

Even if you can't follow a passion or achieve your dream immediately, there's always something you can do in the present – start training or saving the money you need for example – to work towards something you'd like to do in the future. Remember – you've always got options. There are always possibilities.

There's a time for dreaming and there's a time to get started. It's time to get started! Or, as the former governor of New York Mario Cuomo once said: 'There are only two rules for being successful. One, figure out exactly what you want to do, and two, do it.'

Are you willing to do what it takes to create those, including stepping out of your comfort zone? If not, you might consider that comfort is the thing you want most.

Exercise: Think about what you stand to gain

To some extent, working to achieve your goal will be challenging. No one is suggesting you pretend it won't be. But rather than let those difficulties limit you, instead of sticking with reasons not to do it, look for a reason to do it. You only need one reason. You must have a reason to achieve or attain what it is that you want. Why is it so important to you?

On Day 6 you were encouraged to think about what you stood to gain from achieving or attaining whatever it is that you want. Remind yourself what the reason is. Maybe it's a financial or material gain. Perhaps it's personal gain – you'll be happier or wiser, or you will learn something new, be more healthy or improve yourself or your situation in some way.

Whatever it is, write down in your journal why you want to achieve or attain whatever it is that you're aiming for – in what ways will you benefit? What will you gain? Write it down and pin it up where you can see it every day as a regular reminder. Make it a habit to remind yourself of what you'll stand to gain.

Focusing on why you're doing something and what you want to achieve, keeping that in your mind, can help prevent feelings of doubt and uncertainty creeping in, because you're reminded of the positive.

Exercise: Past achievements

Think of a situation in the past when you wanted to achieve something. You put it off for a while but at some point, you did take action.

What helped? What did other people do or say that helped? What did you achieve or attain? In your journal, describe the situation. Then remind yourself that you've got started and reached a goal before. So you can do it again.

Concerns about deadlines

It could be that you're more concerned that you won't have enough time to reach your goal. Certainly, knowing when you want to achieve something by helps focus your efforts. Be careful, though, not to become overly concerned with deadlines.

Although pressure can be positive and motivating, it can also create stress. If you don't meet the deadline or reach your target, you risk feeling like you failed.

Instead of giving yourself a deadline to reach or thinking about how long it will take, know that a step-by-step plan (see Day 11) allows you to work consistently towards what it is you want to achieve, however long it takes. Know that each completed step is a small success and each completed step brings you closer to your goal.

Of course, some goals have an inherent deadline – if you want to learn to dance the tango with your partner for your wedding day, you can't really change the date. What you can do, though, is give yourself a flexible plan to follow – increasing the amount of practice you need – rather than have the pressure of a deadline looming over you.

Remember – you're aiming to think positively. Tell yourself: 'I have a plan. I can manage this.' Just know to focus on one thing at a time.

Change your life today. Don't gamble on the future, act now, without delay.

Simone de Beauvoir

Top tip

Five minutes of positive action: Whatever it is that you need to make a start on, make a deal with yourself: tell yourself you will take the first step today. If, for example, you plan to get fitter, run one time around the block. Instead of putting things off – instead of trying to clean the entire kitchen for example, or arrange every aspect of a holiday – tell yourself you'll do just one thing – take one small step. If even the smallest task seems too hard, make it easy for yourself to get started on the things you do actually want to achieve. If that first step is too big, break it down to a smaller step. Just know to focus on one thing at a time. And each time you achieve a small part of your goal, you get a sense of achievement and see yourself getting closer to what you want.

Popular misconception: you have to wait till you feel like it

More often than not, we wait till we feel like doing something before we take action. We think that if we don't feel like doing it, we won't do it properly and we'll have wasted our time and energy. However, you may well find that once you get started, you end up continuing past the first step.

As Sir Isaac Newton discovered, objects at rest tend to stay at rest. But objects in motion tend to stay in motion. This is just as true for humans as it is for falling apples! When you take the first small step you generate the physical motions, which in turn can trigger the thoughts – the positive thoughts – which correspond to that physical action.

Once you start doing something, it's easier to continue doing it. Take action and things will flow from there. That's why it is important to have a plan for the steps you need to take; it's easier if you know what you're doing first and what step comes next.

Decide what is the one thing you can do right now. Then do that one thing. Send that one email, make that first phone call. Ask that first question. Start filling in that form. Just clear out one drawer. Put just one thing on eBay. Paint one wall. Sign up for that class. Write the first paragraph. Book the flight. Sign up to that internet dating site!

After a short time the positive feelings which you would like from doing that activity start to emerge naturally. You don't have to wait for your thoughts and feelings to change before you get going. Get going and your feelings will change.

Once you understand and accept the logic – that once you get going, you'll feel more positive and more likely continue with what you are doing – it's easier to see what you'll achieve even with the smallest activities for even the shortest time. It's a positive feedback loop – achieving the first small step influences further thoughts and actions.

All sorts of good things can happen once you get started. You have the power. Plug it in!

Make it even easier

Whatever it is you want to do, spend a minute or two setting it up so that it's easier to go forward than to do nothing. Want to go for a swim or a run each morning but can't get your act together? Put your swimming costume or running gear on before you get properly dressed. That way you're far more likely to make a start.

DAY 13

Exercise: Get out of your comfort zone – do one small thing

Just like exercising your muscles to build up your strength, by working on small tasks that you are reluctant to do, you can gain inner strength and develop the ability to overcome your mind's resistance. You can actually train your mind to do what you want to do.

Set small daily goals which you would usually rather avoid doing and get them done no matter what.

Try doing one of these every day for two weeks:

- Make your bed every morning.
- If you take the lift, get out two floors early and walk up the stairs.
- Get off the tube or bus one stop earlier or park your car 10 minutes from your destination and walk the rest of the way.
- Set a timer on your phone for random times in the day. Every time it rings, if you are sitting, get up and walk round for one minute.

When you are able to make yourself do even the smallest things you don't feel like doing, you will feel more in control and pleased with yourself. This can lead to more positive thinking – for example, 'I can make myself walk up the stairs instead of taking the lift every day – that means I can also make myself go to the gym.'

DID YOU KNOW?

If you give meaning to experiences and events – when you see something as an effort and you resist and resent doing things – it's your thoughts about those things that create difficulty. Washing up is just washing up. Cleaning the loo is just cleaning the loo. Making the bed is just making the bed. It is what it is. Neither good nor bad. The same is true of any steps towards your goal. There may be something about it that you don't like. But rather than dwell on it and give it meaning, just do it.

As Shakespeare's Hamlet says: 'There is nothing either good or bad, but thinking makes it so.'

Four ways to get motivated and stay motivated

On Day 7 you read about three things that will help make it more likely that you will achieve any one specific goal: identify the benefits of achieving what you are aiming for, state your goal in positive terms and share your goal with someone you admire and respect. Here are four more suggestions to help you:

1. **Visualize yourself achieving your goal.** Just as you were encouraged to do on Day 9, visualize yourself having achieved your goal. Imagine how you will feel once you have achieved or attained what it is that you want.
2. **Do it with someone else.** If, for example, you want to get a room in your home decorated, invite friends over to help. Then cook everyone a simple meal or order a curry or pizza. Whatever it is, partner up and get it done!
3. **Talk to yourself.** When it comes to persuading yourself about something, research shows that in a variety of situations, if you address yourself by your own name, your chances of doing well can increase significantly. It might seem strange, but it can focus your thinking and motivate you. Rather than telling yourself for example 'I can do this', address yourself using your name: 'Amy, you can do this.' Try it!
4. **Celebrate small wins.** Celebrate your achievements no matter how small they may be. Reward yourself for your progress. Before you get started, think of something you'll reward yourself with as you complete each step.

DAY 13

Key points

- Whatever you want to do or achieve, there will always be something you could point to that's standing in your way before you can fully commit yourself. You can sit and dream, make plans and wait for everything to be just right, but nothing is ever going to happen until you actually start getting on with it.
- Focusing on why you're doing something and what you want to achieve, keeping that in your mind, can help prevent feelings of doubt and uncertainty creeping in, because you're reminded of the positive.
- **Set yourself an intention:** Start doing something! Know that once you do, it's easier to continue doing it; things will flow from there.

Day 14
Identifying and taking advantage of opportunities

INTENTION
To create opportunities and take advantage of opportunities.

THOUGHT FOR TODAY
Luck is what happens when preparation meets opportunities.

Seneca

In terms of abundance, an opportunity is a favourable situation or condition that will contribute towards you achieving or attaining whatever it is that you are aiming for. An opportunity can be a step towards what you are wanting to achieve or it can be the very thing itself. Volunteering, work experience and internships for example are all opportunities to get the skills or experience you need to make it more likely you'll get a particular job. Or the opportunity could be a vacancy for the job itself.

There are two ways that opportunities present themselves: they may be offered to you, but more often than not, you can create opportunities yourself.

Creating opportunities

Don't wait for the right opportunity; create it.
George Bernard Shaw

Once you're clear about what it is you are hoping to achieve or gain, you will need to know what sort of opportunity you are hoping for – what a potential opportunity looks like – so that you can take advantage of it.

Exercise: Move closer to your goal

In your journal, write down what it is you are aiming to achieve or attain. Then think about what would or could help you. What might move you towards your goal more quickly? Would having more money help? More information and advice? More resources? Maybe the opportunity to get more experience would help? Suppose, for example, you were planning to live in Spain next year and you are currently learning Spanish. An opportunity to practise speaking Spanish, before you move to Spain, would most likely be useful to you.

Whatever your goal, just as you did on Day 10 when you were considering your options, this time write down anything and everything that could help move you closer to your goal. Ideas can be realistic or unrealistic – it doesn't matter, because the important

DAY 14

> thing at this stage is simply to imagine all sorts of possibilities. However realistic or unrealistic, however big or small your ideas about potential opportunities, write them down in your journal.

The next step is to actually make one or more of the opportunities that you've identified a reality. How? By thinking of the opportunity as a goal in itself. If we take the example of improving your Spanish, that's now become a smaller goal that's part of your larger goal of living in Spain next year. So, you simply need to take the same approach as you have on Days 10 and 11. Consider your options. Decide on the best option, then take a step-by-step approach to realizing that opportunity. In the example of looking for an opportunity to practise speaking Spanish, you might have a colleague or neighbour who speaks Spanish fluently so you could create an opportunity – ask them if you could practise speaking Spanish with them.

Try it now

Let other people know what you're hoping to achieve or attain. Tell everyone you know. Let them know what opportunities you are looking for. Ask for their ideas – do they have any ideas on anything you can do that would move you closer to what you're hoping to achieve or attain?

Ask people you don't know. Your next opportunity might just be with someone you don't even know yet. You need to find them and go out and meet them.

Top tip

Be someone that other people will want to offer opportunities to. In a variety of situations, show other people that you are willing to go the extra mile. The more you are willing to give to others, the more easily opportunities will come your way.

Being aware of opportunities

Opportunity is everywhere. The key is to be able to spot it. But before you can see an opportunity – you have to be looking for opportunity. This is where your RAS can help you. Once you have identified what you want to achieve or attain and what would make for a good opportunity, you can take advantage of your RAS by consciously using it to alert you to any relevant opportunities that might help you.

You will need to be alert, aware and ready to receive ideas, information and opportunities that could move you closer to achieving your goals. This means you have to be open to new perspectives and ideas that could help you to move forward. Every day, in different situations and circumstances, with what you what you see, hear and read about, consider if there's an opportunity there; an opportunity that will move you closer to what you want to achieve or attain.

Small opportunities count

Small opportunities are often the beginning of great enterprises.
Demosthenes

It won't always be obvious what might help. Opportunities aren't always easily seen or recognized, especially if they are small. But it's not the size of the opportunity that matters; don't underestimate what appears to be a small opportunity, it could very well lead to bigger opportunities in the future.

Spot the right opportunities

Often, when an opportunity comes along, you'll know – your intuition will tell you – that it's right for you and that it's in line with your aims and values. But if you're unsure, you will need to weigh up the pros and cons. Here are some questions to ask yourself:

- Will this opportunity get me closer to my goal? In what way? How will it help me – how will I benefit?

- Is this the right time? If not, will I get this opportunity again?
- Do I have the necessary resources and experience to take advantage of this opportunity? If not, what do I need?
- Are there any drawbacks, any sacrifices I'll need to make? Am I prepared for whatever they may be?
- Are there any risks? Can I manage them?

Step outside your comfort zone: have courage!

Often, opportunities will stretch and challenge you in some way. In a variety of situations, many of the opportunities we come across require us to put in an amount of time and effort. You will need to be willing to step outside your comfort zone in order to take advantage of them, to put in time and effort, to meet new people and have new experiences.

If an opportunity involves an element of risk, think through what you will do if the opportunity doesn't work out as well as you'd expected. As with any decision, ask yourself: what's the worst that can happen? How might I deal with that? If you can answer these questions you will know that you can make a choice and if things don't work out you will already have thought of what to do if things don't turn out as well as you'd hoped.

Fortune favours the bold. So does opportunity. Richard Branson, founder of the Virgin Group, is often quoted as having said that if somebody offers you an amazing opportunity but you are not sure you can do it, say yes. Then learn how to do it later. He's right. Often, an opportunity comes along that's not the perfect time or moment for you – you don't quite have the knowledge, ability or experience. What to do? Tap into your courage! Courage gives you the ability to do something despite any concerns and uncertainty. There is power in doing. So draw on your courage and take action.

Rather than fight feelings of fear and doubt, accept them. Acknowledge your uncertainty, tell yourself, 'I'm not sure about this'. Then push past those thoughts and feelings and tell yourself, 'But I can do this'. Don't overthink it. Often, the more you think about whether you should or shouldn't do something, the less likely you are to take that first courageous step. Courage can be prone to leaking so the longer you wait, the less of it you'll have. Once you've decided to follow up an opportunity, don't wait – do it! Don't wait to feel confident before you do something – do something, learn as you go and confidence will follow.

Managing missed opportunities

Opportunities always look bigger going than coming.
Orison Swett Marden

Imagine you had the opportunity to visit somewhere you've always wanted to go – an event, a show, to see a band you've always wanted to see – or an opportunity comes up that will help move you closer to something you want to achieve or attain. But for one reason or another, you are unable to take up that opportunity. It's a lost opportunity.

A scarcity mindset will see it in terms of 'the opportunity is gone – it will never come along again and I'll never get another one like it'. This is in contrast to an abundance mindset that knows that there are lots of opportunities in life. Yes, that *exact* opportunity may be gone, but others will come up.

Sports fans and people who take part in a sport know that whenever they or their team lose, they can't stay disappointed for long. They know that staying disappointed gets them nowhere. They soon move on to think about the next game or race and the opportunities it will present. In order to leave disappointment behind, you must do the same: make a decision that you are going to move on. It can help to look for something positive about the situation.

If you missed an opportunity to do something because it really was not the right time – you had another engagement, commitment or duty to attend to or you didn't have the skills or knowledge – know that the more of an abundance mindset you have, the sooner you will look for and see the next opportunity.

Yes, in some situations, there may really only be one opportunity. But an abundance mindset isn't about specific opportunities, it's about realizing there will always be more out there, it just may not be the exact opportunity you first encountered. Suppose, for example, a new exciting job role is created at the company you work for. You apply for

DAY 14

the job but don't get it. You think, 'If that role exists, there must be a similar role with other companies. I could even approach similar companies and suggest it to them – actually create a role for myself.' You are seeing options, possibilities and potential: you are thinking with an abundance mindset.

Key points

- An opportunity is a favourable situation or condition that can contribute towards you achieving or attaining whatever it is that you are aiming for. An opportunity may be offered to you, but more often than not, you can create opportunities yourself.
- You will need to know what sort of opportunity you are hoping for – what a potential opportunity looks like – so that you can take advantage of it.
- **Set yourself an intention:** For any one specific goal, know what sort of opportunities would help. Be open, too, to new perspectives and ideas that could help you to move forward.

Day 15
Giving and sharing

INTENTION
To give and to share with others.

THOUGHT FOR TODAY
When you live abundantly and do your best in the world, you lift the tide for everyone else around you.

Jason Marc Campbell

On Day 4, you read about the futility of competing and comparing yourself with others, that looking at the ways in which you don't match up – what you don't have, can't do or will never be – just leads to feeling inferior, disappointed with yourself and resentful of others. Fortunately, nature shows us that there is another approach, one that is not based on scarcity but on abundance and generosity.

In all things of nature, there is something of the marvellous.
Aristotle

The natural world is made up of ecosystems – geographic areas where a wide variety of living things (plants, animals and other organisms) as well as non-living things (the land, the weather, light and dark) interact together as one entity. Every part of an ecosystem depends on all and every other part, either directly or indirectly.

Ecosystems can be very large or very small. Tide pools – the pools left by the ocean as the tide goes out – are an example of tiny but complete ecosystems. At the other end of the scale, the Amazon rain forest is comprised of hundreds of ecosystems, including canopies, understories, and forest floors.

Whatever the size of an ecosystem, each of the diverse species that live there has different needs and each generates resources that they can share. Rather than compete, they evolve to exchange resources with other species. Soil, water, air and sunlight are shared and circulated to maintain all life on earth.

Mature coral reefs and ancient woodland, for example, filled with diverse life, are based on interdependent relationships where resources are constantly exchanged. Not only do all life forms in the ecosystem benefit, but in this way, they all contribute to the wellbeing of the entire ecosystem.

Success in nature is both dependent on and supportive of diversity. Nature shows us that if everyone is after exactly the same resources, they will run out. But by having diverse needs – what ecologists call niche differences – even if only slightly different, we are not all after the same resource: there are only a few of us wanting the exact same thing, so there is enough to go round.

DAY 15

Just like plants and animals, as human beings we benefit from each other's skills and abilities; everything we have, own, use, eat, wear etc is the result of someone else's skills and abilities, time and effort. We can each share what we have in order to give and receive abundance in our own lives; we can circulate the flow of abundance by helping others get what they need.

Non nobis solum nati sumus. (Not for ourselves alone are we born.)
Marcus Tullius Cicero

Common wealth

Speaking on Radio 4's *Today* programme on 23 June 2022, the Rev Dr Sam Wells described the concept of 'common wealth' as rooted in the notion of the common weal, or common good. He references the late MP Jo Cox's words, 'We have far more in common than that which divides us', noting that 'Instead of perceiving wealth as an individual possession, insulating us from society, the term suggests wealth lies in what we share. Common wealth is discovering the myriad things available to us if we open our imaginations to that which belongs to everybody.'

Instead of perceiving wealth as an individual possession, insulating us from society, the term suggests wealth lies in what we share. Common wealth is discovering the myriad things available to us if we open our imagination to that which belongs to everybody.

Exercise: Share what you have

In your journal, write a list of the things in your life that you appreciate and for which you are grateful – your possessions, friends and family:

- Which of these things could you share with others? In what ways?
- When it comes to friends and family, for example, if you haven't done so before, who could you invite to join you at an event or gathering of friends or family? How can you include

other people in the good things in your life? How have you done so in the past?

Next, go back to Day 10 to remind yourself of the skills and strengths that you identified as having.

- In what ways have you used one or more of these abilities and qualities to benefit someone else in the past?
- How could you do so again?

Be kind

Your skills, abilities and knowledge, time and attention, kindness and concern, encouragement and appreciation – all of these qualities cost little or nothing to share and contribute to the lives of others. Let's start with kindness. Kindness involves doing or giving something willingly to assist or lift the spirits of someone else to make their life easier and more pleasant. Kindness comes from a position of goodwill – wanting to do good – do the right, proper, honourable thing – and can make both you and the person you are helping feel good.

Habits are cobwebs at first, cables at last.
Chinese proverb

Exercise: Make kindness a habit

Kind gestures can be spontaneous – holding the door open for someone and smiling at them as you do happens in the moment. So does letting the person who seems rushed go in front of you in the supermarket queue. So does being considerate of other drivers – in a queue, for example, letting people merge in.

Acts of kindness can also be planned: the smallest gestures that don't take too much effort can make a big difference. From

DAY 15

the list below, choose a number of kind gestures and actions you could carry out over the next couple of weeks.

- Make a cake or buy some fresh fruit – summer strawberries, melon or raspberries. It could be for your colleagues, neighbours, family or friends. Surprise them.
- Spread the word. If you know someone who provides a good service – who decorates or cleans, is a plumber or a gardener – and you could recommend them, let others know.
- Do a chore that you don't normally do for someone else. Cook, shop, take the rubbish out, clean the loo, get the car cleaned, change the bed linen.
- Get in touch with someone you haven't been in contact with for a while. Write them a card, email or text just to let them know you were thinking about them.
- Send a surprise gift – a book for example – to a friend. When you find something that's easily affordable that you know a friend would like, don't wait for a birthday or Christmas, give it now.
- Invite people out. How often do you make the first move and ask a friend to do something with you? Is it always the other person that organizes and invites you out? Ask someone to do something nice with you – a film, a show, an exhibition, a pub quiz or a band, for example. Or invite them for a walk, a drink or a meal.
- Save a life: donate blood. Donated blood is a lifeline for many people needing long-term treatments, not just in emergencies. Your blood's main components – red cells, plasma and platelets – are vital for many different uses. Go to http://www.blood.co.uk. Invite a friend to donate with you.
- Save a life: learn CPR (cardiopulmonary resuscitation). If a person has a heart attack, receiving CPR can more than double their chance of survival. In just 15 minutes, you can learn how to save a life. Go to the British Heart Foundation's website and search for 'CPR in 15 minutes'. Invite a friend to learn CPR with you.

> **Top tip**
>
> Pay it forward. If you receive a kindness today, let it be the prompt to do something kind for someone else.

FIVE REASONS TO BE KIND

1. Being kind takes you out of yourself – it opens you up to others and broadens your perspective. In order to be kind, you have to make an effort and be aware of what's happening around you, to be aware of what's happening for other people. When you are focused on yourself, your world contracts, but when you are more aware of others, your world expands.
2. Acts of kindness enable others to feel respected and included, that they are connected to others and that they belong.
3. Kindness is attractive, it makes people want to be around you. When you're kind to people, it makes them happy. The more people who experience kindness from you, the more happy people you'll have in your life. When those around you are happier, your world is a happy place to live.
4. Kindness is contagious. Often, if you are kind to someone, that person and others who see or hear about your kindness are inspired to do something kind themselves. Kindness elevates all who come into contact with it.
5. Being kind to others encourages you to be kind to yourself! You can see yourself as a person of worth, doing the best you can with what you have.

Be generous

Not only can you be kind, you can be generous. Like kindness, being generous involves gestures that make someone else's life easier, less difficult. But being generous means sharing and giving *more* than might be expected. Being generous means giving in abundance.

DAY 15

You have an opportunity to be generous whenever you're aware that extra effort on your part could make all the difference. Although you can be generous with your money and possessions, your time, energy, abilities, skills, experiences, knowledge and lessons learned are all valuable. In fact, all these things are only as valuable as what you do with them, the extent to which you share them with others.

SIX WAYS TO BE GENEROUS

1. **Be generous with your time.** Whether it's ten minutes or an hour or two, spend some extra time with someone who needs it or will appreciate it, someone who is lonely, needs help with learning or understanding something.
2. **Go the extra mile.** Literally. Go out of your way to give someone you know who needs it a lift.
3. **Give more.** Whether it's donating money to a friend's JustGiving page for a fundraising event they're involved in or being your friend's gym partner as they try to get fit, helping someone reach a goal by giving more time or money than they expect is a generous thing to do.
4. **Double it.** If you've never given away money, start by giving away a small amount. Then double it. Buy or cook someone a meal. Then invite some others. Leave a tip. Then double it. Whatever you do or give, do or give a bit more.
5. **Provide the best biscuits.** If you have someone working in your home – an electrician, plumber, builder, decorator, someone to repair the washing machine – offer them more than a cup of tea. Buy some really nice biscuits or cake and offer those too.
6. **Give from the heart.** Giving time, money or effort to something that's important to you – the environment, or a religion, world peace or animal rights – is a good thing to do. Now consider making a contribution of time or money to a cause you have no interest in or connection with but for which you recognize help and support are needed.

> **Top tip**
>
> It's not always easy to remember to be thoughtful and considerate of others. A simple way to remind yourself is to write notes that say 'Be kind' or 'Choose kindness'. Place them on the wall above your desk or on the fridge to remind you. Or make the words 'Be kind' or 'Choose kindness' a screensaver on your phone.

> **Try it now**
>
> Who do you know that's kind? Who do you know that's generous? Spend time with them and learn from them.

The balloons

A teacher gave a balloon to every student. They were asked to inflate it, write their name on it and throw it in the hallway with all the other balloons. The students were given a few minutes to find their own balloon. Despite a hectic search, very few found their balloon. At that point the teacher told the students to take the first balloon that they found and hand it to the person whose name was written on it. In one minute, everyone had their own balloon.

The teacher explained: 'These balloons are like happiness. We will never find it if everyone is looking for their own. But if we care about other people's happiness we'll find ours too.'

Give encouragement, compliments and appreciation

Give what you have. To someone, it may be better than you dare to think.

Henry Longfellow

- **Be generous with your encouragement.** When you encourage someone, you give them the courage or confidence to do something. You might encourage a colleague to apply for a promotion, for example, or you might encourage someone to continue to do something – to cope with a situation despite some difficulties, or to keep training for the marathon or keep going with their studies.

- **Give compliments.** You know what it feels like when someone else says something nice to you – a simple compliment can brighten your day and make you feel good. Whether you've noticed and admired someone's special efforts, something they've achieved, the way they've coped with something or what they are wearing and how they look, don't keep it to yourself. Share your thoughts! Compliments are like gifts, they are not asked for or demanded. But they do make a positive difference. You don't need to worry about getting the wording just right, you simply need to keep in mind that a genuine sentiment phrased a bit awkwardly is better than saying nothing at all.

- **Express and show your appreciation.** Saying thank you not only shows appreciation, it's also an acknowledgement: you've shown that you recognize that the other person gave you their time, energy, or help. When someone else does something for you, express your appreciation to them and explain how they've made a positive difference. Tell them, for example, that their help saved you a lot of time and money. Or that their concern made you feel better.

Feeling gratitude and not expressing it is like wrapping a present and not giving it.

William Arthur Ward

As well as expressing your appreciation, you can show your appreciation. When you show appreciation for something, you demonstrate your gratitude through actions. You reciprocate, you give in return.

Reciprocation can be direct and reflect what the other person has done for you – for example, a friend is there for you when you need to talk to someone about a problem and then when your friend needs someone to talk to, you're there for your friend. Reciprocation can also be indirect – for example your partner cooked, so you wash up. Or your neighbour fixed your bike so you show your appreciation by buying them a bottle of wine. Of course, it's not necessary to keep a score in relationships with family, friends, neighbours, colleagues etc, but often, reciprocating is necessary – it's simply the right thing to do.

WHAT SCIENCE TELLS US

A study conducted by a University of Pennsylvania research team headed by Dr Martin Seligman and published in the journal *American Psychologist* in July 2005 looked at the effects of writing a thank-you letter and personally delivering it to someone who had never been properly thanked for their kindness. The study discovered that participants who wrote the letters were able to immediately experience an increase in happiness scores, with benefits lasting for a month after.

Give it away

If you have much, give of your wealth. If you have little, give of your heart.

Arabic proverb

When you hold onto something that you no longer need, no longer use, or don't like, you're withholding it from someone who *does* need it, could use it, and/or would love it. Whether you give it away or sell it, tell yourself, 'This belongs in someone else's life'. Let someone else use or enjoy the things you no longer use or need.

For it is in giving that we receive.

Francis of Assisi

DAY 15

In the past few years, through Freecycle (www.freecycle.org) I've given away stuff that myself or my family no longer want, like or need. Lego, for example, that our three sons loved and which gave them hours and hours of pleasure – one box of Lego was collected by a woman who sent it to her son working for a children's charity in Rwanda, the other box we gave to someone who took it to a local play centre for children with special needs.

A collection of *Simpsons* comics went to someone who told me: 'My son will be so thrilled when he comes home from school to find I've got these for him.' A didgeridoo that was a gift from a friend went to someone who in his email asking if he could collect it, wrote: 'This would make a great addition to my collection of weird and wonderful wooden objects.' The young woman who asked for the camera I no longer wanted told me she was going to give it as a gift to a friend.

When I cleared out the shed, a spare pair of wellington boots and a garden chair were picked up by someone who'd recently acquired an allotment. The pop-up tent that one son bought for Glastonbury one year was collected by someone else who was off to Glastonbury the following year.

DID YOU KNOW?

Karma – a core belief in a number of Eastern religions, including Hinduism, Buddhism, Sikhism and Taoism – refers to the spiritual concept of cause and effect. With karma, it is believed that a person's actions, thoughts and words will affect them at some time in the future. Like causes produce like effects: a good deed or action will be followed by a benefit or reward of some kind at some point in the future while a bad deed or action will lead to a future harmful effect.

As well as the relationship between actions and consequences, Karma is concerned with the intentions behind actions. If someone commits a good deed for the wrong reasons – they carry out a good deed just to impress others, for example – the action would be considered to produce bad karma.

Karma embraces the concept of reincarnation, meaning that a person is reborn after death: so, a person's karmic sum will decide the form he or she takes in the next life. Furthermore, the good or bad fortune someone experiences in this life may be the result of deeds, actions or thoughts that occurred in their past lives.

What you leave behind is not what is engraved in stone monuments, but what is woven into the lives of others.

Pericles

DAY 15

Key points

- Just as in nature, as human beings we all benefit from each other's attributes – our strengths, skills and abilities.
- The world needs cheerful and generous givers. They improve society. They inspire us. They move us forward. You can be one of them. Be kind. Be generous. Give encouragement, compliments and appreciation.
- **Set yourself an intention:** Choose to do one thing for someone else today – a kindness, an act of generosity. Make it a habit: each day for the next week, think of something you could do – the smallest thing – to contribute to someone else's day.

Day 16
Having compassion

INTENTION
To be open to opportunities to show compassion to others.

THOUGHT FOR TODAY
Be kind, for everyone you meet is fighting a harder battle.

Plato

However much or little you have in your life, when you realize that one way or another, there's always someone less fortunate than yourself and that it doesn't take much for you to make a positive difference, it's hard *not* to do something. It just takes some kindness and compassion.

Compassion is what you feel for a person who has been struck by misfortune; it motivates you to do something to help. Compassion helps you to be aware of the connection you have with everyone.

Popular misconception: understanding what empathy is

You might think that in order to empathize with someone, to feel sympathy and compassion for them, you need to have been in a similar situation facing the same difficulties, or at least be able to picture yourself in a similar situation, facing the same problems. But this isn't so.

Certainly, if you *have* experienced the same difficulties, you will probably find it easier to feel empathy and compassion. But empathy comes from identifying and relating to another person's *feelings* about a situation, not just from the situation itself.

With empathy, even if you can't relate to the experience, you can relate to the emotion (a concept known as emotional resonance). It then follows that having felt empathy, having recognized and understood the emotion that someone is feeling, you can more easily accept how they are feeling – that they are suffering in some way – and show compassion.

It could be, for example, that you don't feel anxious about flying in an airplane, but you *have* experienced anxiety about a different situation. Your ability to empathize then, with someone who is anxious about flying, comes from recognizing, understanding and relating to the emotion – to the anxiety.

In another example, you may not have made the same mistake as someone else but you probably have done something that left you feeling how they do right now – disappointed, for example, or regretful, guilty or worried. These are all emotions that when experienced by someone else, prompt concern and sympathy, kindness and compassion in others.

Compassion and empathy, then, reflect the idea that one way or another, everyone and everything is connected to everyone and everything else.

DAY 16

Being compassionate

Be open to the difficulty, the struggle, the impact of events, the stress, sorrow and strain in others. And respond with compassion. Who today, in your life, could benefit from compassion? Someone who is lonely, unwell, or worried and anxious about something? Someone you know who has recently suffered a loss of some kind?

Be open to compassion for people you don't know: a harassed looking parent, a confused tourist, someone in tears on the bus, on a train or in the street. Moments of compassion come in the flow of life. You can do something small each day to help: a smile, a kind word or a supportive comment can make a positive difference to someone else.

Remember when someone has shown you compassion – they extended a kind, caring concern to you when you were in distress or suffering in some way. What did they do that helped?

What do you think a person who is struggling, who is distressed, might find helpful? Ask them. Ask if you can help. People often find it difficult to ask for help. They feel that they are inconveniencing the other person or being a burden. The next time you know of or see someone who looks down or frustrated, offer to help them. Simply ask how you could help make a situation better.

If you have already thought of something you could do that might help, it might be appropriate to ask first whether they are ok with you helping out in that way.

Try it now

- Be thoughtful. Did your colleague have a bad day today? Bring them a coffee tomorrow morning.
- Cheer up a friend or family member who is feeling down. Find an old photo of you both and get it printed and sent to them by an online photo printing company.
- Get in touch with someone you know who is going through a difficult time or recovering from a difficulty. Phone or write them a card, email or text or send flowers or some other thoughtful expression to let them know you care and are thinking about them.

DID YOU KNOW?

Homeless charities such as Thames Reach, and groups such as the Big Issue, advise people not to give money directly to beggars. So what can you do if you see someone on the streets? Is it compassionate or callous to say hello to somebody huddled in a doorway, but then give them nothing?

Many charities suggest you offer people sleeping rough food or a drink, rather than money. Ask first what food they'd like to receive. Even if you don't give food or a drink, do make some sort of acknowledgement. Don't look away. That's disrespectful. Even if you're not going to give something, make eye contact and say 'No, sorry' because it's at least acknowledging that the person *is* there. In a BBC interview in 2016 a spokesperson for Crisis – the UK national charity for people experiencing homelessness – said: 'Whether or not people give money to beggars is a personal decision, but we know from our own clients how important a simple act of kindness can be to those in desperate circumstances.'

Thames Reach says, 'By all means, engage with people on the street. Perhaps buy them food or a cup of tea.' If you are concerned about them sleeping rough, contact the StreetLink helpline on 0300 500 0914 or the mobile app 'StreetLink' from Apple iTunes/Google Play store or go to www.streetlink.org.uk.

Love is all we have, the only way that each can help the other.
Euripides

Loving-kindness meditation

Some of the earliest Buddhist teachings developed in India emphasized the idea of 'metta' or loving-kindness. The Buddha exhorts 'the good and wise' to spread loving-kindness by making wishes of goodwill towards all beings.

A loving-kindness meditation can help raise your awareness for compassion and empathy. It involves bringing to mind someone you love, and expressing the hope that they are safe, well and happy. You then extend the sentiment to others.

DAY 16

In the same way, we can also draw on the power of prayer. You may pray for someone who is struggling in some way and wish them well, without the expectation that a supernatural intervention will make this so. Instead, a prayer is simply to connect with what that person is going through, being empathetic and expressing concern, care and compassion.

Exercise: Loving-kindness meditation

Bring to mind a person in your life who you care about, someone you like, are fond of or someone you love.

What good things do you wish for them? Your wish for them might be that they are happy, feel connected to others, are kind to themselves, that they are healthy in body and mind. The person you are thinking of may currently be struggling or experiencing difficulties and challenges in their life. So you might wish that they experience healing and wellness, that they be free from fear. That they experience peace and calm. You might wish that someone experiences being loved, supported and encouraged.

In your journal write down whoever you are thinking of and whatever you wish for them.

Now, imagine them sitting in front of you. Focus on your breathing for a minute or two and then, out loud or in your mind, say to this person what it is that you have written down that you wish for them. You might, for example, say about someone who is about to start a new phase in their life: 'May you feel welcomed and included. May you feel understood and supported. May you be content and happy.'

You can extend this loving-kindness to someone in your life who you've had difficulty with in the past or someone you're currently feeling frustrated, irritated or annoyed with. It's not going to be easy, but try to think of something good that you wish for them. It could be that you wish that they have more understanding and patience. Or that they move on with their life. Again, write down what you wish for them and then imagine them sitting in front of you. Focus on your breathing for a minute or two and then, with the same intention and goodwill that you had for the person who you care for, say to them what you wish for them.

If you are charitable, you are rich.

Arabic saying

Know now that regularly practising a loving-kindness meditation encourages an abundance mindset: it opens your mind and heart to be thoughtful and kind, forgiving and compassionate.

Affirmations

Choose one or more of these affirmations, to say to yourself as a reminder that everyone, yourself included, is deserving of kindness and compassion:

- I look to be aware of and support the wellbeing of others.
- I strive to have empathy and understanding for others.
- I look to recognize the emotion someone is feeling.
- I treat others as I would like them to treat me.
- There is often something I can do to make things better.
- I look to make a positive difference to others.

DAY 16

Key points

- Compassion is what you feel for a person who has been struck by misfortune; it motivates you to do something to help. Compassion helps you to be aware of the connection you have with everyone.
- Be open to the difficulty, the struggle, the impact of events, the stress, sorrow and strain in others. And respond with compassion.
- **Set yourself an intention:** Today, think of someone who could benefit from some empathy and compassion. Reach out and show them some compassion. Or place them in your thoughts for a loving-kindness meditation.

Day 17

Being with positive people

INTENTION

To identify and spend more time with the positive people in your life.

THOUGHT FOR TODAY

Surround yourself with people who make you happy. People who make you laugh, who help you when you're in need. People who genuinely care. They are the ones worth keeping in your life. Everyone else is just passing through.

Karl Marx

In his poem, 'People Need People', Benjamin Zephaniah notes our need for people with whom to share experiences, from walking and talking, from kissing to missing.

It's true. People *do* need people. Human beings are social beings: we need to interact with others, to connect and to feel that we belong and are valued. We need *positive* relationships.

Throughout our lives we come across all kinds of people, different in many ways. But when it comes to the impact and influence they have on us – our beliefs, motivation, confidence and self-esteem – other people can often be at opposite ends of the spectrum; they're inclined to either be 'radiators' or they are 'drains'.

People who are radiators spread warmth and positivity: they have an abundance mindset. Drains – people who are more inclined to have a scarcity mindset – can leave you feeling discouraged, disappointed, guilty or resentful. They can drain your energy and drag you down with their negativity.

The story of the tiny frogs

There was once a bunch of tiny frogs, that arranged a running competition. The goal was to run, hop and jump to the top of a very high tower. A big crowd gathered around the tower to see the race and cheer on the contestants.

The race began. No one in the crowd really believed that the tiny frogs would reach the top of the tower. They shouted, 'It's too difficult! They will NEVER make it to the top' and 'Not a chance – the tower is too high'. The tiny frogs began collapsing, one by one, except for those that were managing to climb higher.

The crowd continued to yell, 'It's too difficult! It's much too hard. No one will make it!'

More tiny frogs got tired and gave up. But one continued higher and higher. This one wouldn't give up! And he reached the top.

Everyone wanted to know how this one frog managed such a great feat.

His secret? This little frog was deaf!!

Who you listen to and who you spend time with can make a big difference to your outlook on life. Although you can refuse to listen to other people's scarcity and negativity, it's not always possible or practical to completely withdraw from those people in your life. What you can do, however, is be aware of the effect their negativity is having on you, reduce the amount of time you spend around them and increase the amount of time you spend with the positive people.

Positive people

You need positive people in your life! Positive people – those with an abundance mindset – are likely to respond to you in positive ways and so make you think positively about yourself and your abilities and your potential, other people and the world around you.

It's not difficult to spot positive people. Positive people are people you feel good being around; they're people you can be yourself with. It could be someone you know who supports you when you're down and is fun when you're up. It could be someone who sees your strengths even when you don't. A positive person can recognize the possibilities and potential in themselves, other people and the world in general. A positive person could be someone you know who is open-minded, kind, compassionate and generous. It might be someone you know who is following their dreams; they inspire you.

They might be an optimist – they take a favourable view of events or conditions and expect the most favourable outcome. They are solution focused: they don't get stuck in problems and difficulties, they look for options and possibilities.

Exercise: Identify your positive people

Who are the positive people in your life? In your journal, write down the names of the people who come to mind from the list below:

- Someone I can totally be myself with
- Someone who listens to me
- Someone who encourages me
- Someone who is pleased for me when things go well for me
- Someone I can talk to if I am worried

- Someone who makes me laugh and I can have fun with
- Someone I share an interest or hobby with
- Someone who introduces me to new ideas, interests or new people
- Someone who is generous with their time, ideas or resources
- Someone who has similar values to me.

You may have a different person or a number of people for each situation, or the same one or two people might fit a number of situations. Think widely; the positive people on your list do not just have to be friends or family, they could be colleagues or neighbours. The person you can talk to if you're worried, for example, could be a professional person that you see such as your doctor, a counsellor or someone from a support group. Maybe the person who introduces you to new ideas and interests is a writer or a teacher or someone whose podcasts you like to listen to. Perhaps there's someone on the radio or TV who makes you laugh.

Turn back to Day 6 to remind yourself of your values. Who do you know that shares similar values? They don't have to share all the same values as you – but you may find that those people you know who have very different values from you don't add to your life in any way.

In your journal, add to your list anyone else who has positively influenced your life: relatives, friends, and celebrities, writers and personalities whom you do not necessarily know personally.

Four good reasons to share your goals with other people

The positive people you know are people to talk with about your aims and intentions – your goals – for a number of reasons:

1. Telling others about your aims and intentions makes you accountable. If, for example, you share with a colleague your intention to train to take a different direction in your career, you know that the

next time you see them it's likely that they will ask how your studies are coming along. They are interested. This can help create the incentive and motivation to pursue your goal. Remember, too, the advice from Day 7 – that if you share your goals with someone of higher social status than you, someone you look up to (your manager, a mentor a family member), you are more likely to achieve your goals.
2. During conversations about your aims and intentions, the people you talk with are likely to offer their advice, ideas and insights.
3. Although some will support you, others won't be interested, and others will be sceptical. Talking about your goals will show you who is on your side and who might hold you back. Telling others about your goals helps you identify who your supporters are.
4. When you share your goals with others – for example, details and updates – you are more likely to hear about and meet other people who have similar aims and intentions.

The magical fish

There was once a magical fish that grew in proportion to its environment. At first, it was kept in a pail of water, and only grew a few centimetres. But one day, someone placed the fish in a lake and it grew to measure two metres.

Are you like a fish that has been kept in a pail? When you spend time with positive people, the boundaries of what is possible expand. Which, in turn, gives you the ability to consider new ideas and new possibilities.

Get more positive people in your life

Having good people in your life isn't something that just happens. You have to make time and effort.

If you need more positive relationships in your life, start to meet new people. Think of the things you like to do, such as playing or watching a sport, singing or dancing, painting or gardening – and find people who share the same interests. Of course, making new friends isn't always easy – it takes time and effort; you need to be willing to meet others, to be yourself and give something of yourself. You *can* make new friends but you can't sit and wait for other people to come to you. You need to get out there!

The website meetup.com enables people to find and join groups of other people in their local area who share each other's interests. There are groups to fit a wide range of interests and hobbies, plus others you'll never have thought of. There are book groups, art groups, film and theatre groups and sci-fi groups. Hiking and running groups, football groups, netball groups and cycling groups. People who go to 'Meetups' do so knowing they'll be meeting others who are also open to making new friends. If you find people who are just as keen on, for example, board games, Nordic walking or craft beers as you are, then you'll find it relatively easy to connect and make friends with them. And when you're doing something that's fun and meaningful, your ability to form connections will come naturally.

VOLUNTEER
Volunteering for a cause or local community initiative that interests you is another way to connect with other people and experience positive relationships. Do-it.org is a database of UK volunteering opportunities. You can search opportunities by interest, activity or location.

> **Try it now**
>
> Think about the people for whom you are grateful. Just thinking about them will give you a few moments of pleasure. Express your gratitude to one of those positive people at some point today. Thank those in your life who make it better and happier. Tell them how they make a positive difference to your life and you will get a positivity boost for yourself too.

DAY 17

ROLE MODELS

A role model is someone who inspires you, someone who you admire and want to be like in some way. Supposing, for example, you aspire to financial abundance but believe that getting rich is beyond you, that the odds are against you, that you don't have what it takes to achieve the levels of financial abundance you really want.

And yet, there is plenty of evidence – success stories – that clearly shows us that wealth is a possibility for each and every one of us. Steven Bartlett, for example, is the founder and former CEO of Social Chain, a social media marketing agency. He started the agency in his bedroom in Manchester, England when he was just 22 years old. Five years later it had a market value of over £300 million.

Exercise: Identify your role models

Look for examples of people like JK Rowling, Patricia Narayan, Howard Schultz and Gill Fielding. They are people who have built an abundant, successful life from little or nothing at all. Search for them online and read their stories. Whatever you aspire to achieve or attain – wealth, health, career success, happiness, friendships – look for role models to inspire you.

Look for instances where they demonstrated an abundant mindset. Instances when they:

- let go of limiting beliefs
- visualized what they wanted and how they might get it
- were open to different ways of doing things
- sought out information, took advice and accepted support
- were open to receiving from others
- looked for and took advantage of opportunities
- considered their options
- stepped out of their comfort zone, stretched themselves and took risks
- overcame setbacks
- were persistent and patient.

Then, in your journal, write down what it is about their approach and mindset that inspires you.

Positive news

If you want to fly, you have to give up the things that weigh you down.
Author unknown

Minimize the amount of negative news in your life. While staying up to date can keep you informed and enable you to take part in discussions, it can also mean your life is filled with irrelevant, unnecessary and often distressing information. News and information overload is to the mind what sugar is to the body: empty calories that give you a rush but then bring you down and leave you feeling like crap. You wouldn't want to stuff your body with low-quality food. Why fill your mind with low-quality thoughts?

Read more positive news. Instead of consuming whatever is readily available and drains you, make more conscious choices about what you read, watch and listen to. Watch and read motivational stories or speeches. TED Talks (www.ted.com), for example, are inspiring, educational and motivating.

There are websites dedicated to sharing inspiring and positive news from around the world, for example:

- http://www.dailygood.org/
- http://www.huffingtonpost.com/good-news/
- http://www.goodnewsnetwork.org/
- http://positivenews.org.uk/
- http://www.sunnyskyz.com/

Steer clear of negative headlines and dire tales of the things going wrong. Look instead for uplifting stories that celebrate the best of life and be inspired by the good in the world around us. Read about positive people – ordinary people or famous people – who inspire you.

DAY 17

Key points

- Good people bring out the good in people.
- Positive people – those with an abundance mindset – are likely to respond to you in positive ways and so make you think positively about yourself, your abilities, your potential, other people and the world around you.
- **Set yourself an intention:** Minimize the amount of time you spend with negative people. Identify the positive people in your life and spend more time with them.

Day 18
Being open to receiving

INTENTION
To be open to accepting and receiving.

THOUGHT FOR TODAY
It's better to give and *receive.*

The world is full of options and opportunities, but too many of us come to abundance with a sieve instead of a bowl or a teaspoon instead of a ladle. We don't expect much, and as a result don't get much. A scarcity mindset expects only to receive in the smallest of ways. In contrast, an abundance mindset is open to receiving and expects to receive in a variety of ways – both big and small.

Checklist for receiving

How good are you at receiving? In which of the following situations do you find it easy to receive? Which situations do you find it difficult – feel awkward and uncomfortable – to receive?

- Birthday, anniversary and Christmas gifts
- Thank you gifts
- Gifts that are given to you for no special occasion
- Kind gestures and favours – for example, when someone suggests that they will run an errand or do a chore for you, fix something, collect something, lend you something
- Practical help and support when you are struggling
- Emotional support during difficult situations in your life
- Information and advice
- Compliments and praise.

Children often find it easy to be receptive; they easily accept toys and gifts, praise, love and affection, laughter and fun and all sorts of good things. They simply open their hands and hearts and receive whatever is being offered to them. For some of us though, as adults, we are uncomfortable receiving.

Exercise: Why is it difficult to receive?

Read through the list below. Then, in your journal, write down the reason or reasons why you might find it difficult to accept and receive things from other people.

- I don't feel worthy or deserving.
- I feel like I have to earn whatever I get, that I shouldn't accept something unless I've put in time and effort and worked for it.
- I think that maybe I should give whatever is being offered to me to someone else who needs it or deserves it more than I do.
- I'm embarrassed – I don't know how to respond or what to say.
- I feel the need to give something in return.
- I don't want to be dependent on others.
- I don't want to be beholden or indebted to the person who is giving me something.
- When I give, I feel in control. When I receive, I feel less than.
- It's a responsibility. If, for example, I was offered an opportunity – a promotion – I'd be afraid of failing, or not living up to the expectations of others.

Giving and receiving

Giving opens the way for receiving.

Florence Scovel Shinn

Of course, giving is good but declining to receive the good things in life is not good for anyone. If you are often giving more than you are receiving, you are creating an imbalance. You will have read in Day 15 that nature is the perfect example of the cycles of giving and receiving, that each of the diverse plants and species of an ecosystem has different needs and they each generate resources that they can share. Not only do all life forms in the ecosystem benefit, but in this way, they all contribute to the wellbeing of the entire ecosystem.

Giving and receiving are different aspects of the flow of the circulation upon which everything in nature, including ourselves, depends. If one aspect of this energy flow doesn't function, the circulation of energy becomes stuck and the entire cycle ceases to function. Symbiotic relationships are abundant in nature and are needed for the ecosystem to continue to thrive. Since we are also part of nature, we also need to both give *and* receive.

> **DID YOU KNOW?**
>
> Like yin and yang, giving and receiving are both aspects of the same flow of energy in the world.
>
> Yin and yang – or yin-yang – is a relational concept in Chinese culture. Quite simply, the meaning of yin and yang is that the universe functions as a duality: sets of two opposing and complementing principles or energies that can also be seen in nature. Often, opposing forces in nature actually rely on one another to exist. The nature of yin-yang lies in the relationship and interaction of the two forces. The alternation of day and night is one example as there cannot be shadow without light.
>
> The yin-yang symbol is comprised of a circle divided into two halves by a curved line. One half of the circle is black and represents the yin side; the other side is white and represents the yang side. A dot of each colour sits in the centre of the other's half and represents the idea that both sides carry the seed of the other.
>
> The balance of yin and yang is important, neither side larger or stronger than the other, both integral to the larger whole. If yin is stronger, yang will be weaker, and vice versa. Yin and yang can interchange under certain conditions so that they are usually not yin and yang alone. In other words, yin elements can contain certain parts of yang, and yang can have some elements of yin. This balance of yin and yang is perceived to exist in everything.

Being open to receiving

The saying that it's better to give than receive is, then, untrue. It's better to give *and* to receive. But no matter how much or how often you do or don't give, if you find it difficult to receive by closing off and blocking the good things coming directly your way, you are creating an imbalance. Not only that, but you won't be open to the signs, information and advice, opportunities, support or resources that could lead to an abundance of good things in your life.

DAY 18

IF YOU FIND IT DIFFICULT TO RECEIVE

Receiving *can* come more easily to you; you *can* learn to receive what's offered to you willingly and gracefully. But before you give or receive anything, know that you are enough just by being here. The act of giving or receiving doesn't change this at all. Get into a habit of telling yourself that whatever comes your way, you *do* deserve it. Just by being here. You are just as worthy as anyone else. Rather than play small, be open to receiving more in your life.

Below are some examples of the reasons you might have for finding it difficult to receive. Each reason is followed by suggestions for a more positive approach to receiving.

- **I feel like I have to earn whatever I get. I feel that I shouldn't accept something unless I've worked for it.** Know that although it's always worth putting in time and effort to get the things you want, there's also nothing wrong with receiving something just because it's there or it's being offered to you. Remember, whatever comes your way, you *do* deserve it. Just by being here. You are just as worthy as anyone else.

- **I think someone else needs or deserves what I'm being given more than I do.** Maybe they do deserve it. Or need it. But you can't be responsible for everyone's situation. Of course, if you want, you can invite others to share your good fortune or offer to help them achieve or attain what you have received (you don't *have* to do this though!). And if you really think that someone needs it more than you, then if it's appropriate and won't offend the person who gave it to you, ask the other person if they'd like it.

- **I'm embarrassed, I don't know how to respond or what to say.** Accept a compliment or praise like a gift: just say 'thank you'. It's polite and gracious. All you need to say is 'thank you'. You *can* accept a gift, an opportunity, a compliment or a favour with a 'thank you' and let that be enough. Accepting a compliment graciously tells the other person that you appreciate what they have to say about you. See accepting a compliment as a compliment in itself, that you trust and appreciate their judgement and opinion. If it's appropriate, as well as expressing appreciation, you can *show* appreciation. If, for example, you accept some practical or emotional help, you can do something in return – return the favour or buy a thank you gift for the person who helped you.

- **Accepting something makes me feel beholden or indebted to the other person. I don't want to feel that I have to give something in return.** The other person is offering of their own free will. You're not *making* them give you something, are you? Get over yourself! Accepting something – a lift to work for example, because for some reason you are not able to use your car for the next two weeks – doesn't mean you will become dependent on that person. In a situation like this, most likely, you are being offered something that will meet a specific need at a specific time. Not for the rest of all time. Again, if it's appropriate, as well as expressing appreciation, you can *show* appreciation in some way.

- **When I give, I feel in control, I have a sense of power. When I receive, I feel less.** But that's not fair to the other person. Knowing that giving makes you feel good, it's only right that you give the other person the opportunity to feel good. Isn't it? Accept with grace, be pleased that someone wants to give you something or do something for you. Being overly independent or self-denying denies others the opportunity to contribute and feel good for having done so. Be gracious – accept what someone else is offering. Let others enjoy giving. If you believe that giving is good, why would you not let others do that too?

- **It's a responsibility. If, for example, I was offered an opportunity – a promotion – I'd be afraid of failing, or not living up to the expectations of others.** If you feel that accepting something means that you would have to step out of your comfort zone, that's ok. Rise to the challenge! Rather than worry about failing, get the support, help and advice, acquire the skills and knowledge that you need in order to take advantage of the opportunity that's being offered to you.

Exercise: Conscious receiving

Getting better at receiving, then, is an important intention of abundance. You can make a practice of consciously receiving by acknowledging what you receive on a daily basis from other people. Here are two ways to do that:

- Think about all the service providers that make it possible for you to have water, heating and electric light in your home as well as gas and electric for cooking. You've been the recipient of all these things. Now, out loud or silently, simply say thank you.
- During a meal, choose one food item and think of the long line of people who helped bring it to your table – the farmers, truck drivers, shelf fillers, cashiers, packaging makers. Then out loud or silently, say thank you.

Seven ways you'll benefit from being better at receiving

Whether it's acknowledging what you regularly use as a result of someone else's efforts and abilities, or accepting kind words with a 'thank you', or being let into the stream of traffic and responding with a wave, know that each time you are aware of receiving, you will become more comfortable with receiving and it will become second nature to you. Know that when you are easily able to accept and receive, you:

- believe that you are just as deserving as anyone else of the good things in life
- are more likely to say yes to opportunities that come your way
- are more likely to achieve and attain the things you want and wish for
- find it easier to ask for what you need or want, knowing that you can receive it gracefully and will benefit from it
- show others that you are open and receptive to receiving what is offered to you
- have stronger connections with others
- find that people may give you more, more often!

Exercise: Affirmations for receiving

Choose one or more of the affirmations below or make up your own. Simple affirmations work best because they get right to the point and they're easy to remember. Then, with each affirmation you have chosen, today, in your journal, write it out three times.

You could also write one or more of these affirmations on a sticky note that you put somewhere you can easily see it. Each time you read the words, pause for a few seconds and consider the truth of each affirmation.

- It's better to give *and* to receive.
- I deserve good things, just by being here.
- I am open to receiving more in my life.
- I can receive what's offered willingly and gracefully.
- I can receive good fortune and share it with others.
- When I am offered an opportunity, I can get what I need to help me take advantage of the opportunity.

Regularly check in with yourself using a positive affirmation to remind yourself to be open to receiving.

DAY 18

Key points

- A scarcity mindset expects only to receive in the smallest of ways. In contrast, an abundance mindset is open to receiving and expects to receive in a variety of ways – both big and small.
- Before you give or receive anything, know that you are enough just by being here. The act of giving or receiving doesn't change this at all.
- **Set yourself an intention:** Make a habit of acknowledging something you have received at the end of each day. You could add it to the three good things that you were encouraged to think of and write in a gratitude diary. You will soon find yourself actively looking for things that you have received.

Day 19

Simple pleasures and awesome moments

INTENTION
To include more small pleasures and awesome things in your life.

THOUGHT FOR TODAY
Happiness consists more in the small conveniences of pleasures that occur every day, than in great pieces of good fortune that happen but seldom to a man in the course of his life.
                                                            Benjamin Franklin

As well as working towards achieving and attaining the big things in life, making a point to enjoy life's small pleasures is one of the easiest ways to experience abundance. Small pleasures are the simple things. And there's an abundance of them. In fact, small pleasures are clear evidence that there's plenty of happiness to go round. Because each of us has different things that please us, that give us enjoyment.

What, for you, makes for a small pleasure? Maybe eating the froth on the cappuccino is a small pleasure. Or eating a perfectly ripe pear or peach. Do you enjoy foraging for wild blackberries in the autumn? Perhaps one of your small pleasures is the old comfortable clothes that you put on when you want to relax. What about a bubble bath or a hot shower? Warm towels? Maybe, on a cold morning, it's putting on an item of clothing that's been sitting on a hot radiator? And as odd as it may seem to other people, maybe one of your small pleasures is time spent ironing tea towels and pillowcases?

Small pleasures are woven into your daily life, they are something you can experience at a moment's notice. You just have to recognize them, engage with them and enjoy them.

Exercise: Make a list of small pleasures

Read through this list of small pleasures. Then, in your journal, write down any of the small pleasures on the list that you enjoy.

- Waking up to a tidy kitchen
- Popping bubble wrap
- Lighting a scented candle
- A cup of tea or coffee in bed
- Eating cake
- Wearing a new pair of socks for the first time
- Feeling the sun on your face
- Sleeping in a freshly made bed
- Listening to your favourite songs
- Listening to birds tweeting
- Watching your favourite film or mini-series again
- Wearing an outfit that always makes you feel good

- The smell of toast in the morning
- Making a cake and licking the batter off the beaters of the cake mixer
- Blowing dandelion seeds and watching to see how far they go
- People watching
- Writing with a really good pen
- Slurping hot soup on a cold night
- Sitting in front of an open fire
- Sitting in the sun
- Taking a walk in the rain
- Kitchen dancing
- Car dancing
- Sitting in a rocking chair
- Lying in a hammock
- Singing in the shower
- A lie in
- An afternoon nap
- Reading a book by one of your favourite authors
- Watching the Christmas episode of your favourite sitcom or your favourite Christmas film
- Scrolling through photos of happy times in your life
- A foot massage
- Talking to your dog or cat

Make it a habit

We all have things that please us in some way – that give us pleasure and enjoyment. Each small pleasure, each moment of happiness, is a passing happiness. It happens. And it passes. Life is a collection of moments and the more happy moments we have, the more often we are happy! So make a point of being aware of what's happening around you that pleases you. When you make an effort to notice things, you'll be surprised at just how many things give you moments of pleasure.

In your journal, or on a separate piece of paper, on your phone or other device, add to your list every time you think of something else that brings a small pleasure. Make a list of small pleasures and favourite things, the ordinary and the extraordinary, the familiar and the new, the little things and the tiny things, the cheap and the expensive. And whether they are old or new pleasures, resolve to indulge in them more often.

An inch of gold

There is a Chinese proverb that says 'an inch of time is an inch of gold but you can't buy that inch of time with an inch of gold'. It's true, the smallest events are like gold, they are precious. So enjoy and appreciate the little things, for one day you may look back and realize they were the things that no amount of gold can buy you.

Awe-inspiring moments

Small pleasures are often awesome moments. We all have times when we've been so moved by something – an amazing sunset for example, or a breathtaking view or an uplifting piece of music – that it stopped us in our tracks: we were filled with wonder, admiration and awe. Moments of awe, the combination of feelings – wonder, admiration and reverence – that we feel as a result of experiencing something beautiful, sublime, grand or powerful, are stand-out moments that set themselves over and above the ordinary aspects of our day.

When was the last time you had an awe-inspiring moment? Did anything on the list below move you, fill you with wonder and amazement?

- A view, a landscape or a cityscape
- The power of an ocean, a river or a waterfall
- A sunrise or a sunset
- A piece of music, a beautiful ballad, powerful rock or opera music, an organ recital, music from a symphony orchestra
- A firework display
- A star-filled sky.

Although any one of these experiences is awe inspiring, *any* transcendent phenomenon or happening that goes beyond your ordinary experience of the world can induce feelings of awe and wonder.

DAY 19

Witnessing exceptional ability and skill, acts of courage, bravery, patience, kindness and compassion can inspire awe and wonder. So can being part of a collective act – dancing, singing in a choir or with a crowd. And being part of a ceremony, concert or political march can literally move you.

The arts – visual art, sculpture, music, film, literature and poetry – can fill you with awe and wonder, as can the phenomena of nature, whether it's the delicacy and intricacy of a spider's web or the flowers growing through a crack in the pavement or the abundance of nature – a field full of poppies or sunflowers, for example.

DID YOU KNOW?

Moments of awe and wonder can prompt a shift in your perspective – you become aware that you are more than just yourself, you are a part of a greater whole and something larger than yourself. The sense of connection to something – other people, nature, etc – that fills you with wonder is the essence of spirituality. You might associate the word 'spirituality' with religion, the supernatural and the mystical. But spirituality is simply a sense of being connected to and being part of something bigger and more eternal than both the physical and yourself.

Exercise: Start an awe-inspiring list

Any experience that connects you to something in life that is eternal or larger than yourself – and that inspires you with awe and wonder and moves your spirit – can be a spiritual experience. What do you already do or experience that makes you feel connected? Perhaps it's gazing at the moon and the stars, being outdoors experiencing nature. Perhaps it's playing a team sport or cheering on your team along with thousands of other people. It might be singing in a choir or being at a music festival.

In your journal write down what experiences and situations fill you with awe and wonder. Describe, too, what for you is a spiritual experience, what makes you feel connected to something bigger and more eternal than yourself.

> **DID YOU KNOW?**
> The Varieties Corpus (www.varietiescorpus.com/) is a website where you can share and learn about self-transcendent and awe-inspiring experiences.

Get more Wow! in your life

There's always room for more awe, wonder and connection and there are many opportunities to find them. You just need to be aware of what they are and engage with them. Here are some suggestions for you to explore.

- **Go outside.** Nature – the elements of the natural world, the trees and plants, the animals, the hills and mountains, rivers and other features of the earth – offers so much as a source of awe and wonder. Watching the wind blow through the trees, sensing the power of the sea, gazing at the enormity of a star-filled sky, these are the kind of moments when we can easily experience being part of something bigger, more eternal than both the physical and ourselves. Step back to look at the big picture – the hills and valleys, the landscapes and the views, the rivers and seascapes. Look at the small details – a leaf, a flower, a blade of grass, a shell, a feather, an insect, a spider's web. See them in greater detail. Look for colours, patterns and symmetry. Be aware, too, that nature isn't just in the country, the parks and gardens. It's all around you in the streets and buildings in the towns and cities. Wherever you are, nature is always there.
- **Watch natural history programmes on TV.** These programmes can give you a sense of wonder and appreciation for the world you live in. So can NASA's 'Astronomy Picture of the Day' (apod.nasa.gov/apod/astropix.html).
- **Stop and stare.** Whenever you enter grand lobbies and atriums, churches and cathedrals, mosques and temples, stop and stare. Look up and look all around you.
- **Listen to music.** Make music. Listening to or playing any form of music has the potential to elicit awe – beautiful songs, powerful

lyrics, strong rhythms and beats and full volume – so many aspects of music have the power to move us. Making music with others – be it in a choir, band or orchestra – increases the likelihood of awe because of the synchronicity with other people.

- **Move in unison with others.** Humans have a natural proclivity for synchronized movement. Moving together can move you emotionally. Take part in shared movement such as dance, exercise, or even walking with one or more friends.
- **Take in visual arts and culture.** Visits to art galleries and museums – in person or online – public art and sculpture, and films with stunning visual elements watched on the big screen all have the potential to be awe inspiring.
- **Witness someone doing something amazing.** Be inspired: read or watch films and documentaries about other people's skills and talents or bravery and courage.

Any time you experience something new that moves you, add it to your list of awesome things and wonderful moments.

Key points

- As well as working towards achieving and attaining the big things in life, making a point to enjoy life's small pleasures is one of the easiest ways to experience abundance.
- The small pleasures in life are the smallest of things. You just need to be more aware of them, engage with them and appreciate them.
- Moments of awe – the combination of feelings such as wonder, admiration and reverence that we feel as a result of experiencing something beautiful, sublime, grand or powerful – are stand-out moments that set themselves over and above the ordinary aspects of our day.
- **Set yourself an intention:** Make a list of small pleasures and favourite things. Add to your list every time you think of something else that brings you moments of joy. Make yourself aware of the people, places, experiences and situations that already fill you with awe and wonder. Then, develop that new awareness: commit to experiencing moments of awe and wonder more often.

Day 20
Having patience in the unfolding of events

INTENTION
To be patient in the unfolding of events.

THOUGHT FOR TODAY
  Life is a balance between making it happen and letting it happen.

Often when we think of the situations and circumstances we've had no control over, we think of the unwelcome changes and the losses that we've experienced. But it works the opposite way too: there are often things that are out of our control that actually work in our favour. With the things we want to achieve or attain, there's an element of non-effort; of letting things unfold in their own way and in their own time.

If you've ever experienced occasions when you can't get to sleep, you also know that you can't make yourself go to sleep. Sleep will eventually come, but you can't force it. In fact, trying to make it happen just creates stress and distress which makes sleep even more elusive.

The same is true for many situations in life – just as we can't force sleep we cannot force friendship, love, respect, happiness, forgiveness, success, healing and a variety of other things that we may want to achieve or attain. We can certainly put time, thought and energy into achieving and attaining what we are aiming for but there comes a point where we have to let events unfold at their own pace and in their own time.

Where there is force, there is struggle. Whenever you try to force something to happen, not only are you creating stress for yourself but if it involves compelling and obliging others to do something that they wouldn't have otherwise done willingly, you risk being met with hostility, resistance and resentment. Trying, for example, to make someone cooperate with you, like you or love you, be honest with you or appreciate you is unlikely to turn out in your favour. In fact, if love, respect and appreciation etc are not freely given, you don't really have them.

Time and energy that you put into forcing something to happen are better spent finding a different path, looking for support, opportunities, information or resources that will still allow you to achieve or attain what it is that you want, but in a different way.

Exercise: Work with past experience

Think of a time when you clung onto something, trying to make it work – a job or relationship, for example. Rather than recognize it wasn't working out and that nothing was changing, you hung on in there. Or remember a time when you got lost walking or driving somewhere. Rather than ask someone for directions, you kept going but ended up even more lost.

Whatever the situation, were you calm? Or stressed and agitated? In your journal, describe what happened and what didn't happen. Describe how you felt at the time.

Force versus persistence

To succeed in getting what you want, you'll need to be persistent. But there's a difference between persisting and forcing.

When you're caught up in forcing things to happen it's less likely that you'll step back to see what is and isn't working; you're less likely to think through your options. Instead, you struggle on and close yourself to other possibilities, other ways of doing and achieving something.

In contrast, when you're persistent, although you're determined to succeed with what you want to achieve or attain, you can see when something is not working. You're able to take stock, then adapt and adjust your plans and actions. Rather than stubbornly force things to happen how, when and where you want them to, you're open to new ways of doing things so that you can keep moving forward and get things done.

Acceptance

Forcing things to happen is characteristic of a scarcity mindset. With a scarcity mindset you worry that if situations and events don't happen the way you want them to, opportunities, resources etc will slip through your fingers and so you to try to force things to happen in the way you want them to. But an abundance mindset knows that there are always options – new opportunities arise – they flow.

An abundance mindset can understand and accept that things are or are not happening. Acceptance is not giving in, it's understanding that something is what it is. Acceptance brings a state of calm where you can rest without necessarily needing things to be different.

Once you accept what is or isn't happening, rather than react with impulsive, forceful action, you create a calm space that gives you the time to think things through and act thoughtfully and favourably, to move from force and into the unfolding of events.

A reminder

When you act in harmony with your true self – when what you want is in line with your values, when you are using your skills and strengths to work towards what you want – everything becomes less of a struggle and you can achieve and attain with relative ease. Although there may be challenges, you feel a sense of control; the effort required doesn't seem overwhelming.

In future, when you are working towards achieving or attaining something you want, if you are finding it too difficult and too much of a challenge, stop and consider this: are you simply out of your comfort zone, or are you struggling and trying to force things to happen?

Letting go

It's a fine line between making things happen and letting things happen. It's like trying to remember a place, a name, a particular word. When you stop forcing yourself to remember it – when you let it go – the place, name or word comes to you. Whether it's trying to recall a name or finding the right place to live, the right career or recovering from an illness, to some extent, situations like these unfold in their own time. They require that you accept uncertainty and remain open to possibilities. They require patience.

Popular misconception: patience

Patience, like acceptance, is the understanding that very often, things develop in their own time, that life is a process of unfolding. There's a time for everything and everything takes time.

Patience is often seen as an ability to tolerate and endure under sufferance, to suppress restlessness or annoyance when confronted with delay. But rather than being a state of endurance and reluctant self-control, patience is a state of grace, the ability to experience difficulties and delays, calmly, quietly and steadily.

> ### Exercise: Be aware of impatience
> Often, in a variety of situations, you may not even be aware that you're being impatient because your mind has already jumped ahead to how and where you want things to be. Perhaps, when you realize that something or someone is going to take longer than you'd like, you start looking for ways to hurry things up; you try to get somewhere more quickly, rush an outcome, or make the unknown known.
>
> What are the events, people and situations that often trigger impatience for you? In what situations and circumstances do you try to force things to happen? Write them down in your journal.

> ### Exercise: Practise patience
> Do one activity that requires patience every day for a week and record your progress in your journal. It could be a jigsaw puzzle, sewing, knitting or embroidery, mending or constructing something. Decorate a room. Walk 100 miles. Whatever you choose, notice that little by little, step by step it comes into being, it comes about and is completed.

Reframe the situation

Even when you are aware of being impatient, you might think that the cause of your impatience is specific events or other people that are causing the delay. But actually, the cause is in your own mind – it's your reaction that causes impatience, not what is or isn't happening.

Even though you might not always be able to control how and when things happen, you *can* control how you respond to a delay. From now on, try to recognize when you're becoming impatient. Notice if your mind is agitated – are you feeling irritated, frustrated or annoyed? Is your body tense? Are you fuelling your impatience with judgements about how wrong it all is or how slow things are?

It is what it is. It becomes something that frustrates you only if you attribute a negative meaning to the delay. However long the delay or the wait, it's not permanent. Time always passes, and how you feel during that time is of your own making. Change how you think about a delay and you will have a calmer, clearer mind. See patience as the ability and willingness to let something be, to wait calmly without needing to change it to when *you* want it to be.

Whatever it is that you are aiming for, take stock of your progress – of what you've achieved – on a regular basis. No matter how slow things seem, if you're working towards the next step then you're making progress!

> **Try it now**
>
> Practise being comfortable with sitting, doing nothing. If, when you have to wait, you become impatient or uncomfortable, instead of reading or getting your phone out or huffing and puffing, try just sitting there, looking around, taking in your surroundings. In a queue, just wait in line and watch and listen to what is going on around you. You can even practise patience by *making* yourself wait. Next time, rather than choosing the shortest queue, choose the longest queue. Stand in line and just observe your surroundings and the people around you.

A time for everything and everything in its time

With patience, there is understanding and trusting that things develop in their own time, that life is a process of unfolding. With patience, you know that there's a time for everything and everything takes time. The

DAY 20

following lines are from the King James Bible, chapter 3 verses 1–8 of the book of Ecclesiastes:

> To every thing there is a season, and a time to every purpose under the heaven:
>
> A time to be born, and a time to die; a time to plant, a time to reap that which is planted;
>
> A time to kill, and a time to heal; a time to break down, and a time to build up;
>
> A time to weep, and a time to laugh; a time to mourn, and a time to dance;
>
> A time to cast away stones, and a time to gather stones together; a time to embrace, and a time to refrain from embracing;
>
> A time to get, and a time to lose; a time to keep, and a time to cast away;
>
> A time to rend, and a time to sew; a time to keep silence, and a time to speak;
>
> A time to love, and a time to hate; a time of war, and a time of peace.

In the same way that Christianity recognizes that there is 'a time to every purpose under the heaven', Taoism – a tradition of philosophy and religious belief from ancient China – has a concept known as *wu wei*, which means living with the true nature of the world – without obstructing the Tao (Tao being the natural order of the universe).

Wu wei is a state of being in which our actions and inaction are effortlessly in alignment with the ebb and flow of the natural world. *Wu wei* posits that there's no need to try to make things happen, instead, we just go with the flow, patiently letting things be and trusting that things will take their natural course in the same way that a river flowing through the landscape finds its natural course.

Taoism encourages us to live a life of balance and harmony; we can still be proactive but our actions fit into the natural pattern of the world.

Taoism encourages us to live with patience and trust. It suggests that we are judicious – we use good judgement – with our physical, mental and emotional energy, knowing that things will eventually come into being. *Wu wei* shows that when we do less, when we wait and watch, we see outside influences and phenomena more clearly and make wiser moves.

> ### Try it now
>
> Taoism suggests we develop our understanding of the concept of non-action by observing the natural world. One way you could do this is to plant some bulbs – daffodils and tulips in the autumn for example, or gladioli or acidanthera in the spring. They will sit in the ground for many months but then in their own time, they will appear out of the earth and come into flower. A reminder that, trusting that everything is as it should be, there's a time for everything and everything in its time.

Affirmations

Affirmations help remind you of how you want to be and what you aim to become. Today, the aim is to develop patience in the unfolding of events.

- I can wait calmly without needing to change it to what I want it to be.
- Time always passes. How I feel during that time is of my own making.
- Trust that things develop in their own time. Life is a process of unfolding.
- There's a time for everything and everything takes time.
- Everything is happening as and when it should.
- All is for the best in this best of all possible worlds.

Key points

- Patience is a state of grace, an ability to experience difficulties and delays quietly and steadily with fortitude and calm.
- Taoism and Christianity both suggest that rather than force things to happen, often we just need to go with the flow, to patiently let things be, trusting that things will take their natural course, that there's a time for everything and everything in its time.
- However long a delay or the wait, it's not permanent. Time always passes, and how you feel during that time is of your own making. Change how you think about a delay and you will have a calmer, clearer mind.
- **Set yourself an intention:** Practise being patient. Starting today, do one activity that requires patience every day for a week. And, next time you have to wait in line, rather than choosing the shortest queue, choose the longest queue.

Day 21
Managing setbacks

INTENTION
To manage setbacks and keep moving forward.

THOUGHT FOR TODAY
Things will work out best when you make the best of how things work out.

It's likely that as you work towards something you want to achieve or acquire, problems will arise. Whatever you wish for, whatever you're aiming for, things happen. It could be that financial difficulties or health problems crop up. Perhaps other people block you or deny you in some way. You might, for example, get turned down for the place on the course or the job you were relying on getting as a step towards the career you want. Maybe you make a mistake – perhaps you underestimate how much time or money you'll need to achieve your goal.

Whatever goes wrong or sets you back, it doesn't have to be the end of the road. Yes, it's upsetting, disappointing or frustrating but rather than let a setback completely discourage and demotivate you – instead of letting it drag you down into a spiral of negativity – think in terms of abundance: identify what options and possibilities you now have that will enable you to continue working towards what it is you are aiming to achieve or attain.

Acceptance and commitment

On Day 3 you were introduced to the concept of acceptance and commitment as a way to move on from negative unhelpful thoughts to more empowering thoughts. An acceptance and commitment approach can also help you manage difficulties and setbacks. With an acceptance and commitment approach, whatever has gone wrong, you acknowledge and accept that what has happened has happened and nothing can change that. You acknowledge and accept what is beyond your control.

You don't pretend you're not upset, disappointed or frustrated, you acknowledge and accept you feel like you do. But rather than get stuck berating yourself or blaming and railing against someone else, rather than give up, you acknowledge the disappointment, hurt, frustration etc. You accept that you feel like you do. Then you move on – you commit yourself – to what positive steps you can now take.

Supposing, for example, you didn't get the house or home you were hoping to buy or rent – maybe the house sale was subject to closed bids and someone else offered more than you. Or the seller or landlord decided to withdraw their property from the market. Whatever the reason, you are upset. But rather than dwell on how, why, why not, you'd *accept* that what's done is done. It's in the past. You'd then look to see what, if anything, you can learn from the situation. And then you would consider what your options are and you would *commit* to what you can do from now on, to move forward in a positive way.

Acceptance and commitment recognize that when you accept what happened and let go of negative unhelpful thoughts, you let go of the emotional aspects of a situation and allow the rational, logical part of your mind to start working for you, to think in more helpful, practical, positive ways.

Moving forward

We must embrace pain and burn it as fuel for our journey.
Kenji Miyazawa

You may remember having read on Day 14 that sports fans and people who take part in a sport know that whenever they or their team lose, they can't stay disappointed for long. They know that staying disappointed gets them nowhere. They soon move on to think about the next game or race and the opportunities it will present.

In order to leave disappointment behind, you must do the same: make a decision that you are going to move on. It can help to look for something positive about the situation.

Exercise: Reflect on past disappointment

When was the last time that you were disappointed? What did you learn? Did you even stop to reflect on this? Think back to challenges and setbacks from the past. Think about how you overcame those.

In your journal, describe a situation where, despite difficulties and a setback, you still achieved or attained what it was you were aiming for. Describe:

- what you were aiming for
- what went wrong

- what help and support, if any, you received from other people
- how things eventually turned out well.

Next, think about and write down what strengths and qualities and skills and abilities helped you manage the situation. You might notice that, for example, your ability to be decisive, to make decisions easily, with little hesitation, or your sense of humour played an important part in overcoming the difficulties and moving on.

If you are currently experiencing a setback, consider how you can apply those same strengths and abilities and get help now. Think, too, who could help and support you.

Having options

Imagine you are planning a car journey: you're going to drive somewhere 200 miles away. You've looked at your options – the different routes you could take to get there. You've decided what the best route is and you set off. All's going well but after 50 miles there's a traffic jam and they've closed the road ahead. Or you get a puncture. Or maybe the motorway service station you planned to stop at for a meal is closed. What to do? Do you give up? Of course you don't. You identify and assess your options and you decide what you're going to do next.

It's the same approach with setbacks to anything you set out to do: you identify what, exactly, the problem is and then you look for a solution. You might be able to deal with the problem or you might conclude that Plan A isn't, after all, going to work out. So you create a Plan B. In fact, if, when you were thinking through how to achieve your goal, you identified some options for achieving that goal (as you were encouraged to do on Day 9), you will already have identified an option that could be your Plan B.

When you really want to get what you want, there's always a way. And most likely, there's more than one way. As we said above, 'If Plan A doesn't work, the alphabet has 25 more letters.'

DAY 21

A reminder

On Day 11 you were encouraged to anticipate problems and difficulties that might occur when you are working towards something that you want to attain or achieve.

Thinking about what could go wrong – what might be the worst that could happen – is not to discourage you and put you off doing what you want to do. On the contrary, it's making it more likely you'll be successful because you've anticipated the potential problems and you've already thought through how you might deal with them.

Six steps to managing a setback

1. Identify what exactly has gone wrong. Is this a temporary setback, or something that changes everything?
2. Assess the situation. What, if anything can you learn from this? What might you do differently in a similar situation?
3. Decide if you need to adjust your goal or change direction. If so, what are you aiming for now – a different goal or the same goal?
4. Decide what your options now are.
5. Having decided on what direction and what option to now take, decide what your first step will be. And the next step. And the next steps.
6. Get going!

Be inspired by others

Whether you got turned down for the course or the job or a TV talent show or another business got the sale you were trying to make, there will always be other possibilities. This is something that the writer JK Rowling discovered. When her first submission to a publisher of *Harry Potter and the Philosopher's Stone* was rejected, she submitted it to 11 more publishing houses before the publishers Bloomsbury accepted it.

Anyone who has succeeded or achieved something has faced some setbacks. But they stay open to possibilities and move forward. And sometimes that may have to be in a different direction. Sir Paul Smith, the fashion designer, left school at 15, intent on becoming a professional racing cyclist. But, at 17, he was involved in a serious accident and was in hospital for several months. During his recovery, he made some new friends, who introduced him to art, design and photography. He was inspired, and realized there were new possibilities, a new direction for his life. He enrolled onto evening classes for tailoring and with the help of his then-girlfriend (now wife) and a small amount of savings, he was able to open his first shop in Nottingham in 1970. He was still only 24. By 1976, Sir Paul was showing his first menswear collection in Paris. He has since gone on to open shops in London and New York, as well as showrooms in Milan, Paris and Tokyo.

In 2013, when workmen botched the job of building her new home and left her £160,000 out of pocket, it seemed that Carol Sullivan's hopes of transforming her bungalow had been dashed. Faced with having to demolish her home and unable to pay someone else to put things right, Carol decided that the way forward was to build the house in Kempshott, Hampshire, herself. She enrolled on a bricklaying course, learned the basics of plumbing, electricity and carpentry and began constructing a four-bedroom property from scratch. Carol put her job as a divorce lawyer on hold to get up at 6am and spend the day laying bricks from Monday to Friday, with her husband helping her at weekends. A year to the day from when she started, they moved in and continued to complete the house. Apart from getting workers in to do the roofing, levelling the concrete and the plaster work, Carol did everything else including the plumbing to the electrics to the carpentry.

In his 2005 Stanford University graduation address, Steve Jobs explained that although it didn't seem like it at the time, getting fired from Apple was the best thing that could have ever happened to him. He explained: 'It freed me to enter one of the most creative periods of my life.' Over the next five years, he started a company named NeXT, another company named Pixar, and met his future wife. All of which, he told the audience, wouldn't have happened if he hadn't been fired from Apple.

At the 2016 BRIT music awards there was much criticism about the lack of black nominees and winners. Funk singer songwriter

George Clinton had a different perspective. 'It's always been that way,' he told the BBC, 'but it only makes you have to work harder and get better. That's what it takes to become great: adversity. Things are always changing for the better. Fault is easy to find – but finding a reason to keep on pushing is the hardest thing. And when I can find that reason, I'm satisfied.'

When things don't go the way you hoped they would, you might need to adjust your expectations but that doesn't always mean that you have to lower your expectations. A few years ago, I was writing articles for magazines and I had an idea for an article on the subject of resilience. I pitched it to several editors but none of them was interested. Once I'd got over my disappointment, I decided that even though magazine editors weren't interested in my idea, book editors might be. Together with my friend Sue, I approached publishers and we were commissioned to write our first book. I've since written more than 20 books, for both adults and children.

> **Top tip**
>
> It's too easy to remain unhappy if you're still attached to how things 'should' have been or 'should' be. These expectations are characteristic of a scarcity mindset: they are disempowering because as long as you're trapped in them, they are preventing you from acting constructively on your situation.

A fall into a ditch makes you wiser.

Chinese proverb

With an abundance mindset, you focus on thinking about what can be done rather than what can't be done, and you are open to new ideas and new ways of doing things. Rather than thinking, 'I should/shouldn't have ...' try saying 'It might help to ...' or 'I could ...' or 'Now I'm going to ...'.

Ask yourself, 'What can I learn from this?' and 'What will I do differently now?' Focus on learning and improving. Focus on what can be done rather than what can't be done; be open to new ideas and new ways of doing things.

Being persistent

Often, when things get difficult, it's easier to give in and give up. But as someone once said, 'You didn't come this far to only come this far.' You need to persist!

As you read on Day 20, when you're persistent, although you're determined to succeed with what you want to achieve or attain, when problems crop up, you adapt and adjust your plans and actions. With persistence, periods of difficulty are interspersed with small gains and measures of progress. These small gains can inspire you and give you hope; you can recognize and build on the small gains.

> **Exercise: Persistence**
> Think of a time when you've achieved something through persistence – passed your driving test, learned to speak a language, to play a musical instrument or some other skill. No doubt it wasn't easy but you achieved it because you were persistent: when things became difficult, you found a way to overcome the challenges and you moved forward. In your journal, describe what happened, what the difficulties were and how you eventually achieved what you were aiming for.

Without persistence, not only do you achieve less than you're capable of, you don't get to discover what you *are* capable of achieving. And you don't get the confidence that comes from pushing through and eventually succeeding. Persistence provides its own momentum. If you can find a pathway through to what it is that you want and you just keep going, you'll eventually get results. And results motivate you to continue, to achieve and attain more.

DAY 21

Keeping motivated

On different days in this book you've been encouraged to identify and remind yourself of the good reason for pursuing your goal. After a setback, reminding yourself of how you will eventually benefit from continuing to work towards whatever it is you are aiming for can encourage you to get back on track. So can visualizing. On Day 8 you read that the future you see is the future you get. So make a point of visualizing yourself managing the setback and successfully achieving what it is that you wish for.

Don't forget to reach out for support and encouragement from other people, from friends, family, colleagues, or professionals. Let others know when you need help. If they don't offer, then ask. Even if the person you ask can't help you, they may have some suggestions as to how best to cope or who else might be able to help or advise you.

And finally, know that as frustrating as things might be right now, the situation *will* change, life will continue and one way or another, things *will* work out. As you read on Day 20, rather than force things to happen, you may need to patiently let things be, trusting that things will take their natural course.

Key points

- It's likely that as you work towards something you want to achieve or acquire, problems will arise. Getting stuck in how things 'should' have been or 'should' be is characteristic of a scarcity mindset: it is disempowering, preventing you from acting constructively to deal with your situation.
- With an abundance mindset, you focus on thinking about what can be done rather than what can't be done. You are open to new ideas and new ways of doing things. You know that whenever you are able to adapt, you create the possibility of happiness and success that doesn't depend on perfect conditions.
- **Set yourself an intention:** Whenever you experience a setback, remind yourself of how you successfully managed a difficulty in the past. Be inspired, too, by other people's experience of managing a setback and going on to achieve and attain what they were aiming for.